INTERACTIVE WHITEBOARDS
in the
ELEMENTARY CLASSROOM

Tony DeMonte

International Society for Technology in Education
EUGENE, OREGON • WASHINGTON, DC

INTERACTIVE WHITEBOARDS
in the ELEMENTARY CLASSROOM

Tony DeMonte

© 2013 International Society for Technology in Education

World rights reserved. No part of this book may be reproduced or transmitted in any form or by any means—electronic, mechanical, photocopying, recording, or by any information storage or retrieval system—without prior written permission from the publisher. Contact Permissions Editor: www.iste.org/learn/publications/permissions-and-reprints.aspx; permissions@iste.org; fax: 1.541.302.3780.

Director of Book Publishing: Courtney Burkholder
Acquisitions Editor: Jeff V. Bolkan
Production Editors: Lynda Gansel, Tina Wells
Production Coordinator: Emily Reed
Graphic Designer: Signe Landin
Proofreader: Kathy Hamman
Indexer: Wendy Allex
Cover Design, Book Design, and Production: Kim McGovern

Library of Congress Cataloging-in-Publication Data

DeMonte, Tony.
   Interactive whiteboards in the elementary classroom / Tony DeMonte.
     pages cm
   Includes bibliographical references and index.
   ISBN 978-1-56484-330-2 (pbk.)
   1. Interactive whiteboards. 2. Teaching—Aids and devices.
 3. Education, Elementary. 4. Educational technology.   I. Title.
   LB1044.88.D46 2013
   372.133—dc23

                     2013009025

First Edition
ISBN: 978-1-56484-330-2 (paperback)
ISBN: 978-1-56484-480-4 (e-book)
Printed in the United States of America

Cover Art: © Dreamstime.com: Aldegonde Le Compte, Karam Miri, Lucadp, Asbestosmatt
Inside Art: © Dreamstime.com: Asbestosmatt

ISTE® is a registered trademark of the International Society for Technology in Education.

About ISTE

The International Society for Technology in Education (ISTE) is the trusted source for professional development, knowledge generation, advocacy, and leadership for innovation. ISTE is the premier membership association for educators and education leaders engaged in improving teaching and learning by advancing the effective use of technology in PK–12 and teacher education.

Home to ISTE's annual conference and exposition and the widely adopted NETS, ISTE represents more than 100,000 professionals worldwide. We support our members with information, networking opportunities, and guidance as they face the challenge of transforming education. To find out more about these and other ISTE initiatives, visit our website at www.iste.org.

As part of our mission, ISTE Book Publishing works with experienced educators to develop and produce practical resources for classroom teachers, teacher educators, and technology leaders. Every manuscript we select for publication is carefully peer-reviewed and professionally edited. We value your feedback on this book and other ISTE products. Email us at books@iste.org.

International Society for Technology in Education
Washington, DC, Office:
    1710 Rhode Island Ave. NW, Suite 900
    Washington, DC 20036-3132
Eugene, Oregon, Office:
    180 West 8th Ave., Suite 300
    Eugene, OR 97401-2916
Order Desk: 1.800.336.5191
Order Fax: 1.541.302.3778
Customer Service: orders@iste.org
Book Publishing: books@iste.org
Book Sales and Marketing: booksmarketing@iste.org
Web: www.iste.org

About the Author

Tony DeMonte is employed as the coordinator of instructional technology for Zion Elementary School District 6, in Zion, Illinois. In that role, he guides the district on instructional technology decisions and oversees the technology department as it pertains to educational and infrastructure needs. He has presented workshops on the topics of early literacy, integrating technology with young learners, interactive whiteboards, and assessment systems. He has served as an assistant principal in an elementary school and a kindergarten teacher for several years. He holds a certificate in administration and supervision from Dominican University, an MEd in technology in education from Lesley University, and a BS in elementary education from Northern Illinois University.

Dedication

To my wife, Kelli, for supporting my passion of integrating technology into the lives of young learners. This passion sometimes carried into areas of our personal lives, and I thank you for your love and understanding; and to Katie Jones, my mentor teacher and friend, who helped form my teaching style and philosophy of education as I watched her make every minute of school purposeful and challenge all students to make academic gains regardless of their starting points.

Contents

CONTENTS

INTRODUCTION

The interactive whiteboard (IWB) has revolutionized the way elementary educators deliver instruction. This easily viewable, touch-board technology not only brings a wealth of information and resources found online into the classroom, it allows teachers to take that information and make it interactive and engaging. Whether a teacher is referencing online resources or using the IWB software for notes, diagrams, or other activities, this is a powerful teaching and learning tool.

The effective use of IWBs has also changed the way that students feel about learning, increasing their engagement, achievement, and motivation. Elementary-aged students learn best using a multisensory approach. An interactive whiteboard provides a medium for students to see, hear, and touch the learning material. Interacting with learning material keeps the students engaged through a lesson over the length of a school day or a unit spanning multiple days. When teachers use an IWB's capacity to present information in differentiated ways, students with different learning styles flourish. Use of an IWB can increase student achievement by meeting the students' individual needs.

Interactive whiteboards also positively affect student motivation. When students are presented with material in ways that are understandable, they enjoy the learning process more. When they use an IWB, students feel excited about school because they can be involved in the learning process. Understanding, enjoying, and being engaged in the material motivates students to come to school, encourages participation, retains student interest, and increases their willingness to follow teachers' directions.

When this book speaks of *interactive whiteboards*, this term broadly encompasses the many different types and configurations of a technology that displays an image that teachers and students can interact with without using a keyboard or mouse. It refers to all brands of interactive whiteboards, whether the software offers only a few tools or many bells and whistles. The board can be a hard surface or a soft, roll-up version, it can be mounted on the wall or on an adjustable-height cart. There might not be any board at all, just an interactive projector that turns the wall or a dry-erase board into the interactive surface. Even interactive TV screens are included in this type of technology. The important thing is that teachers understand the capabilities of their IWBs and have access to resources that support their teaching. The goal of this book is to provide some of those resources to elementary education instructors.

An interactive whiteboard is a tool that adds value to any classroom activity. I believe that every elementary classroom could benefit from having an IWB. The field of education can arguably benefit from this tool becoming a stock item in every classroom for a variety of reasons that will be explored in this book.

Using this Book

This book is divided into three sections. Part One, Meet Your Interactive Whiteboard, reviews the basics of interactivity, hardware, and software.

Part Two, Discover the Benefits of Interactive Technology, looks at the benefits that effective use of an interactive whiteboard can bring to your classroom. These benefits include increased student engagement, greater student motivation, and differentiation to meet varied learning styles.

Part Three, Explore Lesson Ideas and Resources, features resource listings, tools, and ideas that you can put to work to help integrate your interactive whiteboard into your classroom effectively. This practical guide details how to transition what you are already doing in your classroom to the interactive whiteboard. It also provides lesson "sparks" in language arts, mathematics, science, and in other areas. The language and math sparks are correlated to the Common Core State Standards (CCSS). If you're looking for more lesson resources and ideas, this section guides you to resources offered by equipment manufacturers, other educators, and education organizations that have found the best ways to engage their students using the interactive whiteboard.

PART ONE

MEET YOUR INTERACTIVE WHITEBOARD

Touching on Interactivity

The most important thing that separates an interactive whiteboard from a marker board or projector is interactivity. For the purposes of this book, interactivity means that users can control what happens on the display (screen) by operating it like a giant touch screen. The level of interactivity can vary from device to device and depends on the software used with the device. An example of basic interactivity is a teacher displaying his or her computer desktop on the board and asking students to locate and start the web browser by using the whiteboard pen to mimic a computer mouse. More advanced interactive features include the capacity for multiple students to interact at the same time, motion-sensitive input, and even voice activation.

Any interactive whiteboard can work with the programs loaded on a connected computer. For instance, an IWB can show a drawing program running on a connected laptop and allow users to draw using that program. Virtually all of these systems can communicate wirelessly with a computer, and many can also use a wired connection. Several types of interactive whiteboards can perform some functions on their own. For example, many interactive systems include their own drawing program built into the operating system of the whiteboard, so you can use the whiteboard interactively without a computer being connected. Some IWB systems include extensive built-in capabilities, rivaling the power of a separate computer.

Touch-sensitive IWBs. Many of the stand-alone whiteboards include electronics within the whiteboard surface. The most expensive of these are fully touch sensitive: Interactivity can be achieved with virtually any touch. These whiteboards tend to be relatively rugged because the device doesn't have to house the actual display (the display is projected onto the board). Because these boards are almost always paired with a closely integrated projector, they don't need to be calibrated and are very easy to start up.

Pen- or stylus-based IWBs. Another category of interactive white-boards are the pen- or stylus-based interactive systems. Basically, these devices include the electronics in a pen or other pointer that comes with the board. These pens almost always require batteries. Although some systems automatically calibrate the projected image and pen location, typically you'll need to touch the four corners of your whiteboard with the pen at least occasionally to calibrate the image and pen locations. Some systems require this calibration every time you start up. Interactive projectors nearly all use the pen- or stylus-based interactive system.

Touch-screen monitors. The newest interactive technology working its way into schools is a large touch-screen monitor or television. Although some feature computing power within the monitor, some of these require a separate computer with either a wireless or cable connection. These devices are still relatively expensive but have multiple advantages: They are extremely easy to use, they are immune to shadow effects because there is no projector, and they have excellent picture quality. But perhaps the biggest advantage is that this technology does not require special pens or pointers. You can use a finger (or a nose!) or a basic pointer to achieve interactivity. Of course, overly aggressive touching or hitting can damage the display, and some devices are more damage prone than others. Glare can also be an issue with this type of interactive display.

Hybrid IWBs. Many hybrid combinations of these interactive whiteboard systems exist. Sometimes there are electronics in both the board and the pens. This allows for a smaller, less expensive pen, sometimes without a battery. Some systems will allow multiple pens to be used at once. There are also a variety of ways in which the pens (if needed), board or display surface, and computer communicate with each other. Although wireless capabilities can safely be assumed, speed, cost, and utility can vary considerably. For instance, infrared technology is inexpensive and uses relatively little battery power, but it requires a somewhat short line-of-sight distance between the pen and the computer or projector it is communicating with. Bluetooth (a wireless communication standard), on the other hand, is more expensive and generally discharges batteries more quickly, but it has great range and can communicate without direct line of sight. For permanent installations, cabling's superior bandwidth may be the preferred option because wireless solutions may not be able to handle high-resolution video. If you plan to use your interactive display to show DVDs or Blu-ray movies, you'll want to check that the link between your computer and display device is capable of doing this.

IWBS IN ACTION

If you're looking for a basic interactive whiteboard demonstration, you can find lots of videos on YouTube. Here are three suggestions to get you started:

Interactive Whiteboard Demonstration (4 minutes)
www.youtube.com/watch?v=DjdNPMZJbLs
(http://bit.ly/3wlVO)
A social studies teacher demonstrates how an interactive whiteboard works.

Interactive Whiteboard Teacher Training (9:32 minutes)
www.youtube.com/watch?v=75-7UqTy040&feature=related
(http://bit.ly/eOrK9p)
A basic introduction to using interactive whiteboards in the classroom is shown.

Kindergarten Interactive Whiteboard Use (5:11 minutes)
www.youtube.com/watch?v=RYulh2IduDk&feature=related
(http://bit.ly/12rvZcs)
A kindergarten teacher takes her class through a word family lesson on the whiteboard.

Teachers can be interactive with students using technology in many ways. Even though the more expensive systems may be well worth the money, it is important to remember that even the most rudimentary interactive system will provide all the benefits and learning opportunities discussed in this book. For the most part, the difference is going to be how much extra preparation and planning that you, the teacher, will need to contribute.

Anatomy of a Whiteboard

Interactive whiteboard systems traditionally include three hardware components: the board, the projector, and a computer.

The board (or hard surface) component of the interactive whiteboard system is more than just a simple surface; most whiteboards from the big companies contain electronic components inside. The boards sometimes have pen trays attached that hold the special pen(s) necessary to use with them. If you think of a traditional SMART Board or Promethean-brand board, this type of interactive whiteboard, with electronic components inside, is what probably comes to mind. Hitachi StarBoards, PolyVision, Panasonic, Mimio, and other manufacturers also offer versions of this type of whiteboard.

The boards with electronics inside tend to be more expensive than the alternatives, but they are usually the most sensitive to user input, and they may be truly touch sensitive (no pen needed) and feature-rich. Many are totally wireless and can accept input from a variety of sources. Some include the facility for a teacher to choose the display from among a number of computers, video devices, tablets, and other devices, such as student "clickers." These IWBs often have internal capabilities that allow them to be used in a variety of ways without a separate computer attached. This alone may make them more popular because teachers do not need to dedicate their classroom computers to whiteboard activities.

Integrated Systems

The most common type of interactive whiteboard right now is the wall-mounted, hard-surface board with an integrated projector. If you walk into a classroom with one, you would see a board mounted on the wall with some type of attached arm that extends out and holds the projector. If the arm, also known as the *boom*, extends about 3 to 4 feet, then the projector attached to the arm is known as a *short-throw projector*; the image is thrown onto the board surface from a short distance. Sometimes the arm is shorter or even nonexistent. If the projector is mounted directly on the wall and extends 1 foot or less, you have an *ultra-short throw projector*.

Either a short-throw or an ultra-short throw projector will display the image satisfactorily. However, the shorter the throw, the fewer problems there will be with shadowing. Remember film strips or movie projectors found in classrooms a couple generations ago? What happened when students walked in front of the screen as they went to their seats? You saw their shadows on the screen instead of the picture. The same holds true for an interactive whiteboard. The farther out the projector, the more shadowing can occur from the teacher's hand or body. To minimize shadowing, the best choice is an ultra-short throw projector. However, these projectors tend to cost more because of the types of lenses and mirrors inside the device.

Integrated systems can be mounted on a wall or mounted from the ceiling. Mounting an interactive whiteboard onto the wall is the simpler option. Often no additional hardware beyond the bracket that usually comes with the board is needed for wall mounting. When mounting from the ceiling, however, additional parts, such as brackets, cylinders, and long cables, may need to be purchased, and installation may involve adjusting ceiling tiles.

For powering either type, an electric outlet is needed in the vicinity of the projector. Tracks, ties, and hooks can easily hold cables along the wall, and if installation is done correctly, they can be hidden around the existing chalk or marker boards.

Most integrated interactive whiteboard systems communicate with the teacher's laptop or desktop computer using wireless networking technology. But sometimes (especially with older models) you'll need to connect the whiteboard to your computer using cables.

The biggest benefit to a wall- or ceiling-mounted board is permanence. Assuming the board was placed with considerable forethought (see Location, Location, Location! on page 16), you won't need to stop your lessons to bring in and set up equipment, nor will you need to reconfigure students' desks and chairs. Of course, this permanence could also be a slight disadvantage in some cases because you lose the flexibility of moving the whiteboard to different areas depending on its use.

Split Systems

In some interactive whiteboard systems, the board and the projector are separate units that can be configured in many different ways.

The projector can sit on a table or be ceiling mounted. Placing a projector on a table is the least desirable location because tables in classrooms get moved and bumped. Whenever the projector is moved, the board will need to be recalibrated. This process, although easy, can become bothersome if it must be performed multiple times daily. Additionally, projectors are expensive and easily the most fragile part of an interactive system, especially when the projector lamp is running or has recently been on. So leaving a projector on a table or desktop where it is vulnerable to damage could be a costly mistake.

Ceiling mounting is the traditional way of installing a projector. One benefit of this installation is that the projector is out of the way and out of the reach of students. Another benefit is these types of projectors cost less if a standard model is purchased. The downsides of a ceiling-mounted projector are more opportunities for shadowing due to distance and a dimmer image. The farther away the projector, the brighter it will need to be in order to project the image, especially in classrooms that need to stay lighted. Projectors are rated in brightness by a lumen rating; the brighter the projector, the higher the lumen rating. Everything else being equal, the price will go up with the lumen rating, thus increasing cost, depending on how bright it needs to be. Overall, traditional projectors tend to be somewhat more affordable than wall-mounted ones or ones integrated with the whiteboard, but extremely bright (high lumen) models function well in well-lit rooms and can project a large display.

Another consideration for mounting on a ceiling is ceiling design; such mounting may not be an option, depending on the type of ceiling. For instance, ceilings with beams instead of tiles pose an installation challenge. Some older buildings have additional older ceilings that exist well above the visible ones. In these cases, special mounting plates are needed to help the projector hang properly. So projector installations on ceilings need to be done on a room-by-room basis based on the ceiling construction. This attention to installation holds true for integrated systems as well as for split systems.

Portable Systems

In some education systems, a number of staff are displaced every year due to building overcrowding or classroom reconfiguration. If an interactive whiteboard is desired in this type of continually displaced environment, a portable option, such as the ones listed below, may be appropriate.

Stands. Hard-surface boards do not have to be mounted on a wall. The big IWB companies all sell stands that hold their equipment.

This system is ideal when wall space is not available. For example, some schools designed in the 1970s with an open-school concept have no or few internal walls. This design enables the inside learning areas to be reconfigured yearly, depending on class size and how many sections of a grade level are needed. Likewise, an interactive whiteboard stand can be moved as needed. The greatest strength of a stand, portability, is also a downside. The stand needs to be heavy and secure so that it does not tip or become a safety hazard.

Rollable carts. Rollable carts, usually designed for a specific brand of board, can hold hard-surfaced boards and projectors. Some of these can be raised and lowered using their own hydraulics. The portability of these carts means they can easily be moved and shared between classrooms. To minimize setup, having a dedicated laptop on the cart makes it its own self-contained unit. Don't let a lack of knowledge of the equipment or the seemingly long setup time stop you from using a cart. It's important to reach out for training on how to set up, turn on, and configure these systems. Knowing exactly how to set up the cart will increase your skill at doing so, lessen the setup time, and, in general, make you more comfortable with using the board.

One of the most valuable features of carts is the ability to adjust their height to match the height of the students. For students who are physically challenged, bringing the board down to wheelchair level allows them the same access to the board as their peers. Unfortunately, rollable carts can be quite expensive.

Soft-surfaced boards. Soft boards are attached to the wall with magnets or double-sided tape. The technology does not reside in the soft board as much as it does in the pen that is used with it. The pen, driven by Bluetooth, becomes the more expensive piece of equipment of the entire unit. Some soft-surfaced boards can be rolled up and put inside a carrying case to be transported.

Sensor attachments/Capture technology. Some interactive whiteboards have little to do with the board itself. Separately attached systems or capture technology can be an affordable way to interact with a surface. These system attachments clip or stick onto the wall or existing marker board. Mimeo boards are an example of this technology. The biggest benefit is cost. Not only is the infrared or sonic technology less expensive; it also has fewer components to ship and install; consequently, there are fewer parts to break. If the surface gets damaged, the sensors can be moved to another surface.

Interactive Projectors and Displays

Some interactive whiteboard systems have no boards at all: Interactive projectors are new to the classroom scene. An interactive projector has an additional component that builds interactivity right into the projector and the pen. Epson, BOXLIGHT, InFocus, Dell, EIKI, Hitachi, SMART, and other brands offer their own versions. The largest benefit to this option is cost: Aside from the projector, the pen is typically the only other device required. The second biggest benefit is the projector's facility to use any other interactive software with it, provided that the appropriate licensing is purchased. In addition, an interactive projector can be easily adjusted for the teacher's and students' heights by changing the tilt of the projector. No mechanical adjustment needs to be made to accommodate the people using it.

Interactive projectors do come with a fault, although it is relatively minor: The surface projected onto needs to be flat and smooth. Cinderblock, brick, and many typical classroom walls with uneven textures may not work well with an interactive projector. The pen will respond to the bumps on such walls, and the image will have a wobbly appearance. Smooth drywall can be damaged over time using this type of system. The best-case scenario for an interactive projector is projecting onto an existing white marker board. The next best is melamine board or other smooth surfaces purchased from a hardware or big-box store. Boards usually come in 4-by-8-foot sheets and can cost less than $10 apiece. Some interactive projectors have the option of a special mount so they can be turned vertically on a table; then the table surface becomes the interactive area.

Also new on the education scene are interactive displays—LCD flat-panel televisions or monitors that have touch capabilities. The upside to these is the ease of installation: They mount just like a flat-panel home television. There is no need for a projector and no shadowing effect. Interactive displays do tend to have higher upfront costs than other interactive solutions, but total cost of ownership may be similar to other interactive board solutions, considering there are no projector bulbs to replace. The downside of interactive displays is the relatively small size of the display. If students in the back of the classroom can't easily read from the device, this system loses much of its interactive advantage. As sizes increase and costs continue to decrease, however, these interactive televisions and monitors should become viable options for more and more classrooms.

Whatever form your IWB takes, it needs to work in your space and for your day-to-day teaching functions. If you have influence on the choice of an IWB, look for a system that can withstand the rough conditions of constant use. No matter how slick the design or innovative the technology looks, the system must be user-friendly enough to be naturally integrated into the classroom.

Interactive Whiteboard Software

Good software can go a long way toward making the IWB useful to both students and teachers. Not all the bells and whistles are needed, but they can help. The more flexibility that the software allows, the more teacher creativity can shine through. The larger interactive whiteboard manufacturers offer in-depth, constantly updated software that is more than just marker color, eraser, and shape creator. The additional functionality of these IWBs adds the wow factor without requiring much time for the teacher to create the wow.

Software evaluation by educators should be just as important as physical hardware evaluation by a technician. Good software can ease the pressure on staff in lesson preparation and can excite students so they are engaged in the learning process.

As previously mentioned, any interactive whiteboard system can run programs from a connected computer. For example, you can launch Windows on your computer, open a paint program, and draw away. There are virtually unlimited options—open the browser on your Macintosh, surf to a Web 2.0 photo-editing site, and start editing, for example.

These are great options, but you may want to explore some software that takes advantage of your particular whiteboard. Many valuable whiteboard-specific resources you can tap into can be found in Part Three: Explore Lesson Ideas and Resources. Most IWB systems come with software that includes extensive templates, clip art, and teaching materials. For instance, virtually every inter-active display system comes with digital maps. These are generally available in a variety of formats, they are easily resized, and they can be customized for specific purposes. Some digital maps are even animated. For example, you could pull up a spinning globe, open to the continent you are on, then to the region or state you are in, and then maybe even to a county or city map.

Location, Location, Location!

This mantra is used by retail stores to emphasize one of the most important factors in a business plan. Likewise, the location of an interactive whiteboard in a classroom space can make or break its success. Occasionally interactive whiteboards are installed in locations that don't necessarily make instructional sense for the students who use them. Sometimes a board is installed in a spot for no better reason than that is where the network drop or electrical outlet is located. Whiteboards should not be installed for the ease of maintenance or for technology department needs without consideration for the instructional needs of the students the board will serve.

It is important for teachers who have interactive whiteboards (or will be getting one) to thoughtfully consider the location of the board. If the whiteboard in your classroom is in a poor location, you will need a specific, well-thought-out justification for why it needs to be relocated. If you are getting a new interactive whiteboard, you will want to figure out from the beginning the best location for instruction and interaction. Aspects of location to consider are board height, wall location, instruction area and ease of student access, lighting, and computer location.

Board height. In a primary classroom, height of the interactive whiteboard needs special consideration. Whether the board is on a mobile adjustable cart or is installed low on the wall, students must be able to reach every part of the board; the shortest student should be able to touch most of the board. Where low installation is not possible due to electrical outlets or to building design, the whiteboard can be raised slightly, and a sturdy step or mini stage installed for students to use.

One of the downsides to a step or stage, however, is student accessibility and safety. For physically challenged students, rolling a wheelchair up to the board or negotiating the steps may present a problem. This can be partially remedied by using a pointer. Sticks, swords, rods, and other pointers used for interacting with big books also make handy touching tools with an interactive whiteboard, provided your board does not require a special pen. If it does require a special pen, check to see if the manufacturer sells one with a longer reach.

Wall location. If your IWB is not on a cart, then determining where on the wall it is installed should entail the same logic used in determining where a marker board, chalkboard, or screen gets placed. The length, or wide, side of a classroom allows for the greatest number of students to easily view the whiteboard and sit closest to it. Placing the board at one end (the "short side") of a room can present a problem for any students in the back row trying to read text.

Instruction area. The whiteboard should be located near an area where the group meets for other activities. If instruction is done on a carpeted area, the board should be placed within that carpeted or circle area because there is a higher probability that students will then naturally use the board in activities. Think about a one-computer classroom: If the computer is located near the carpet area, in a center or station space, or on a student-sized computer table, it will have a higher likelihood for use than if it resides on a teacher's desk or in a spot where it needs to be pulled out for use. A bad location, such as behind a teacher's desk or podium in an old science classroom, can inhibit traffic to the board.

Lighting. Natural and artificial lighting impact how well the image can be seen on a whiteboard. Almost all classrooms are naturally lit well, with large or many windows common in most schools. However, the brightness of the sun can create a glare, thus a washout effect on the board. This is especially true if the board is installed perpendicularly to the window wall. Before a whiteboard is installed, special thought should be given to how the room is lit during all times of day and all times of the year. To reduce glare, the board should be installed as far away from windows as possible.

To help students see the IWB's images more clearly, a brighter projector may be needed. However, the brighter the projector, the more it costs, and the less likely your school may be able to afford it. Blocking the natural light and dimming the artificial light can be the cheaper solutions. Aside from equipping the room with blinds or shades, block natural light with what is within your means, such as moving the furniture strategically. Bookshelves, old mobile chalkboards, file cabinets, and easels make good visual blocks. You can reduce artificial light easily if your lights are on banks so that you can turn off one line of lights but not all or turn the direction of the light fixtures to redirect where the light shines. See the following diagram for good IWB placement.

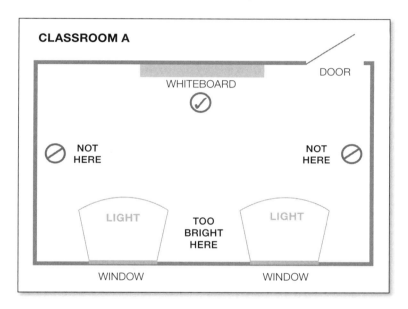

Pay close attention to where the projector shines in relation to the ceiling lights. If a bulb is located above or between the projector and the board, it may have a washout effect on the image. A simple solution here, if maintenance or facility staff cannot move fixtures, would be to remove the bulbs from the lights directly above the projector and the board. Having too much light, natural or artificial, adversely impacts the majority of boards on the market. The location of the board in relation to lighting is just as important as other placement considerations.

Computer location. If possible, the computer connected to the board should be near the front of the class alongside the board. Young students have short attention spans, and asking a group of young learners to wait while the teacher moves across the room to type something on the computer may cause a loss of momentum in a lesson. Being able to turn instantly from reading a story on a chair, to the computer for typing a website address, to the board itself for interacting with an online activity can mean the difference between a successful lesson and one with distractions that require the teacher to refocus students' attention.

Sharing options. Due to budgetary constraints, some schools have opted for their interactive whiteboards to be mobile and shared. A similar situation occurs when projectors are checked out from an AV department, library, or computer lab. However, sharing this type of technology comes with a cost, and that cost is time. No matter how few cables or how simplified the process, you have to spend the time to bring the IWB to your classroom, set up the technology, and possibly troubleshoot problems. Lack of time, lack of access, and discomfort with the equipment can deter IWB use.

If you have to share an IWB, consider having one teacher "own" or house the board. Having one person responsible for it will ensure that it is properly set up and maintained and that at least one person will know how to accurately troubleshoot problems. You should also work out a scheduling system with your colleagues to ensure access for everyone and to avoid situations where the IWB is kept without being returned. If a projector or interactive whiteboard permanently resides in one nearby classroom, the speed of accessing it and the synchronization with your immediate colleagues can encourage its use. If you "own" the equipment and can count on it being there, you can better spend your time researching ways to use the IWB with the curriculum.

Although it is nice to consider everyone's feelings, placing an IWB permanently in one room with a teacher who is properly trained and excited to use it may create a higher likelihood for the board's use. This doesn't mean that other teachers cannot use it, but it does mean that they may need to swap rooms for a lesson, co-teach, or use the interactive whiteboard at a time when that other class of students is somewhere else. The IWB's lack of mobility does not necessarily mean limitation on who can use it.

Even if you are satisfied with where your interactive whiteboard is located, think about whether you should relocate it to allow for more student "customers." Successful retail stores look to increase sales by moving their stores, or products within their stores, to better locations. As many students as possible should be served by the board. Open floor space around the board for student gatherings and small-group work is just as important as height, wall location, or permanency considerations. Using the board as a center or station for whole-group instruction allows for more students to be served throughout the duration of the school day.

Think location, location, location!

PART TWO

DISCOVER THE
BENEFITS OF
INTERACTIVE
TECHNOLOGY

If you are lucky enough to have an interactive whiteboard in your classroom, ask yourself if you are using it to its full potential. Is it a teacher tool or a student learning resource? It can and should be both. Using an interactive whiteboard effectively can bring many benefits to your classroom: increasing student engagement, enabling differentiated instruction and scaffolding, assisting with classroom management, promoting best use of limited resources, allowing shared learning, increasing student achievement, motivating students and teachers, and helping teachers meet technology standards.

Student Engagement

Teachers commonly state that today's generation of students needs substantially more engagement to sustain their attention than did previous generations. The reason that students need more engagement may be due to physiological changes in their brains.

Psychologist Aric Sigman (2010) suggests that the immediacy of interacting with computers, gaming consoles, and cell phones results in higher levels of dopamine, a chemical that contributes to learning and concentration, being released in the brain. Students who regularly access information by way of screens, with their fast-paced and visually stimulating environment, may have trouble with concentration because their brains have become desensitized to normal dopamine levels, making it difficult to concentrate on nonscreen-based stimuli. Although research into this topic is minimal at this point and sometimes even contradictory, it could explain why some teachers feel the need to change their teaching methods to make their lessons more interactive and lively. Effective use of an interactive whiteboard can feed this need for engagement and fill the requirement for how younger students now learn.

Active learning strategies, such as those involving interactive whiteboards, have been shown not only to increase student attentiveness during the actual activity but to have an extended effect afterward (Bunce, Flens, & Neiles, 2010). In other words, inserting activities with the whiteboard into your lessons not only improves how your students pay attention and learn during the activity, but it will help them keep their attention on learning throughout the school day. Another interesting finding from the study was that the effects of active learning strategies are not limited to just the students directly involved. Even those students who simply observed other students interacting with the whiteboard also demonstrated heightened attention and learning motivation that lasted throughout the school day.

Rather than needing to find ways to encourage students to use the whiteboard, you will need to find ways to select from the students volunteering to use it and to make sure all have opportunities. Some teachers have reported volunteers being so many and excitement being so high that they have to find methods to choose among the students who want to use the whiteboard. Some IWB software comes with random name generators to help with this process, but the traditional methods of selecting students, such as choosing a tongue depressor with a name, randomly choosing a student number, or selecting someone wearing a certain color, can all work. This is a far cry from the days of students not raising their hands and hoping that the teacher does not call on them.

Differentiated Instruction

In my opinion, "sit-and-get learning" (the teacher-centric model of learning) should only be read about in history books and displayed in museums as the way we used to teach early elementary grades. Thanks to Gardner's (1983) theory of multiple intelligences and other research, we now know that young students learn in different ways using different methods. Meeting the learning needs of all students means diversifying the methods of delivering content. Pedagogy influenced by multiple intelligences theory is much easier to implement with an interactive display. The flexibility of both the input and output of an interactive display enables a teacher to easily incorporate lessons that use spatial, musical, naturalistic, and other key intelligences that are difficult to incorporate in a classic sit-and-learn environment. Obviously, interactive whiteboards are also a great tool to help foster inter-activity, another of Gardner's intelligences.

Interactive whiteboards are invaluable in implementing differenti-ated instruction (DI) strategies based on learning styles in your classroom. The flexibility and multimedia aspects of interactive displays naturally lend themselves to presenting material in diverse and reinforcing lessons. Using an interactive whiteboard provides an avenue for students to interact with information in different ways. For instance, one lesson could focus on students writing or solving simple mathematical equations, such as $2 + 1 = 3$, much like in the traditional classroom. The next day, the same math concepts may be shown by having students drag digital "leaves" onto numbers to solve the equations.

Engaging as many senses as possible during a lesson will ensure that most learning styles are addressed. If students have reduced sensory inputs or if they simply learn better with one style rather than another, then compensating by focusing on strength areas will help them achieve the greatest success. Know your learners!

Six Learner Types Helped by IWB Use

Following is a list of some of the predominant means by which students learn and the advantages of the interactive whiteboard in meeting these specific needs.

Visual learners. The IWB allows teachers to add visual elements, such as digital photographs, clip art, and video clips to their lessons and to make the best use of visually rich, web-based games and activities. Visual devices, such as diagrams, graphic organizers, charts, tallies, or any marks to accentuate a point, can be drawn on the IWB to make connections to patterns or relationships. Writing or drawing on top of an image or text, highlighting passages, or underlining words can all be ways to spotlight key terms or ideas during a lesson. Videos, slides from a presentation, or visual puzzles can retain a student's interest in the content. Students can, in effect, become like the computer mouse, interacting with visual messages. Visual learners can be engaged by these and many other IWB activities.

Subscriptions to video libraries can be purchased, giving teachers access to videos that can supplement social studies or science concepts. These supplements not only add relevant video clips into a teacher's tool kit, but they do so with proper licensing, which is well worth the cost.

Auditory learners. Including sound recordings, sound bites, or sound effects in a study unit helps meet the needs of students who are primarily auditory learners. For these students, combining audio and visual representations helps form stronger connections in the brain, allowing them to better remember the material. Sound files for subject material ranging from presidential speeches to animal sounds are easily found on the Internet.

Text-to-speech software, which can read the letters, words, or sentences, and narrate the text aloud, can be helpful to auditory learners. This functionality is usually included as an acces-sibility tool in the IWB software found on systems built by the large manufacturers. Imagine a class of first graders working on sight words. Those students can interact with a sight word using paper letters, worksheets, or writing slates. Those same activities displayed on an IWB can help reach auditory learners if every time the word is touched, it is read aloud.

Teachers can help auditory learners by capturing their lessons through IWB screen-recording software and a microphone and making the recordings available to students outside of class. For example, seeing and hearing recordings of explanations of how to solve math problems, class discussions, and trivia-based games being played can help auditory learners review the lessons that were taught in the classroom. If posted to the web, these demonstrations can not only help students after school, they can help families support learning beyond the school's walls.

It is important that the sounds are clear and loud enough for the entire class to hear. For this to happen, the IWB system should include external speakers connected to the computer or mounted speakers connected to the board. The type of speaker is not important as long as the hardware is properly installed and the sound quality is high.

Kinesthetic learners. Kinesthetic learners often benefit the most from an interactive whiteboard. Touching an IWB to reinforce how a letter, number, or shape is drawn can provide as much help as when younger students do the same using sand or shaving cream. Thus, interactive whiteboards that allow touch using a finger, fist, or palm are of most benefit to kinesthetic learners.

The board should not be reserved for just small-motor movements. Use of the board should be expanded to achieve full motion and extension in a young learner's hand and arm. Letters and numbers can be written extra-large to fill the size of the board. These larger movements involve more muscles and help students feel the motion with their entire bodies. Manipulating cubes or rulers, or flicking images in the midst of a game increases students' touch sensations, heightening their awareness of the lesson content.

Students with visual impairments. For students with visual impairments, including auditory elements and actions involving touch will help them learn concepts that usually are taught mostly visually. If students are learning how to draw a shape, the student who is mildly visually impaired can benefit from a thicker or darker line color, a larger shape, or a filled-in solid shape to make the image more noticeable and to have better contrast. The student can also hear the teacher and students speak about forming the shape. Recording the lesson will allow students to play back that recording for future practice. Touching the interactive whiteboard while forming the shape provides tactile input, allowing students to feel the lines and turns. The repetition of movement can help to solidify the shape in their brains.

Students with hearing impairments. Students who have hearing difficulties benefit greatly from the visual nature of the interactive whiteboard. Those visual strengths of the board help balance their other areas of need. Directions can be typed or written on the board before, during, and after the lesson to reinforce verbal instruction. Whether students understand what is being said by lip reading or through sign language, the same process can be used at the board that is used in other areas of the classroom.

Students with learning disabilities. Teachers who work with students with learning disabilities are accustomed to providing assistive technology and classroom supports in order to help students learn the material. Examples of these supports include using a ruler or other hard-edged surface to help students read line by line, highlighting words or parts of a word in different colors, or writing down multistep directions to help students remember the order in which to work. All of these supports can be provided through the interactive whiteboard. The more robust the IWB software, the easier it will be to provide these supports naturally within the lesson. Writing out the steps on the board; using different colored pens, markers, and highlighting tools; and using shading tools or lined paper can assist students who learn by separating content.

Scaffolding

Interactive whiteboards are extremely good when used in *scaffolding*, a critical component of successful teaching in early-elementary education. Scaffolding is a teaching method where, with guidance from the teacher, students build on prior knowledge to gain skills. At a basic level, automatic shape and pattern generators can help students express themselves and work toward mastering concepts, even when their drawing or writing skills may still lag. The support provided by these tools allows students to learn the concepts faster. Eventually students should transition away from the tools to demonstrate skill attainment without the supports in place.

For example, you could use scaffolding with an IWB in a science lesson on the water cycle. The IWB lesson template could have arrows, boxes, photos, and drawings that could be moved to the correct location to show the order of the water cycle. Below the template could be text descriptions to explain the concept further. The teacher could reference the text and guide the students to move pictures to their correct locations. After students demonstrate mastery of the concept, the template could be changed to take away text, arrows, or even the pictures. The students might be asked to manipulate just the pictures or words or asked to draw or write the water cycle on a blank screen without any supports.

Well-done scaffolding can also be used as an assistive technology. From the more obvious strategies, such as expanding content on screen for visually impaired students, to less obvious strategies, such as including audible clues, interactive displays make good teaching practices easier. In some cases they allow teachers to innovate and reach students in ways never before possible.

Classroom Management

Even if you're a bit hesitant to explore new pedagogies and methods, interactive whiteboards can still be powerful tools for classroom management. Physically active students may be much less disruptive if they are given the opportunity to move around and interact with the whiteboard. Likewise, you may choose to reward students by giving them the pen to lead the class. Because of the technology's appeal to students, it can be used quite effectively as an incentive. In addition, virtually all interactive display systems come with software to enhance classroom management, including basic tools, such as countdown timers, roll-call lists, and other attention-getting features.

The interactive whiteboard can be used as a behavioral management tool. Some students need constant reminders to stay on task and complete work in the assigned time. Visual timers can help support students who need that cue to stay focused on the task at hand. A countdown clock from the web or a clock graphic from the whiteboard software can be displayed on the board. A variety of timers, including more visual ones that represent time left, may help students who cannot read numbers.

For loud groups of students, a purchased "noise meter" can track the decibel level in the classroom by way of computer microphone. Students are asked to keep the noise level below a specific point. For the entire class, a game could be used to symbolize a threshold. For instance, a picture of a baseball diamond and scoreboard could be displayed. As the batter circles the bases, rewards are won. A "three strikes and you're out" rule could mean a student or the class loses a privilege.

Creative positive behavioral incentives can be used on the IWB. For example, as the students follow class expectations, a piece to a puzzle could be added that will eventually show a picture of a prize. Or a virtual marble jar, smiley chart, or pictures of a thumbs-up could be moved and tallied as goals are met.

Interactive whiteboards can be used for a multitude of teacher management tasks. Seating charts with students' names can be easily moved around on an IWB to group students differently. Classroom jobs can be identified on the board. Using random student generator graphics, such as dice or spinners, can be helpful when the teacher needs to choose a volunteer.

Leveraging Limited Resources

Classrooms are generally equipped with at least one computer for keeping electronic attendance, for gradebook programs to track progress, and for checking teacher email, among other uses. But prohibitive cost has stopped some schools from purchasing two or more computers, tablets, and other portable technologies per classroom. For schools with limited resources, having an interactive whiteboard can open the access of that one computer to the entire class for whole-group instruction or for smaller groups at centers, stations, or group-work time. What can be seen as a large initial cost to a school board can also be viewed as a wise investment in making sure that the one computer is used to its fullest extent.

Shared Learning

The format of using an interactive whiteboard in a whole or small group creates a dynamic of shared learning. Communicating and collaborating is necessary because by design the board is not a one-person tool. The students not only become involved with the board and learning, they also become involved with one another. Learning becomes verbal and reciprocal. And explaining, reasoning, and discussing solutions are critical to deep understanding.

Many mathematics programs in the primary grades are now emphasizing the explanation of how to figure out answers rather than just focusing on the pure calculation. If students can show how they derived an answer by explaining the process to the teacher or a fellow student, it demonstrates a deep level of knowledge. When young learners become involved with one another in this way, these conversations help deepen their level of understanding of the content. Shared learning with meaningful and relevant discussions among students can only happen when the students are involved.

Student Achievement

Too often the latest technological gadget, subscription program, or piece of software is seen as a tool that can increase learning just by appearing in the classroom. That could not be further from the truth. The same holds true with the best-written basal reader or science experiment kit; these tools are only as good as the teachers who use them. Likewise, having an interactive whiteboard in the classroom alone will not increase student achievement, but paired with a highly competent, skilled teacher, it will very likely increase student achievement.

One of the largest studies of students using interactive technology, including whiteboards, was conducted by Robert Marzano (Marzano & Haystead, 2009). This multiyear study found that in classrooms using interactive technology, student academic performance increased 16 percentile points. The findings showed that gains were made across all student populations, across all levels of teacher experience, and across all subject and grade levels. Student performance improved immediately with interactive whiteboards and increased with use.

In all fairness, it must be noted that this particular study was conducted in classrooms that used additional interactive technology, such as student response systems, software, and learning communities in conjunction with the whiteboards. But the interactive whiteboard was at the center of the research. This research also concluded that adequate professional development in teachers is critical. Greater student gains were noted when their teachers were more confident using the technology.

Another notable study of IWBs was conducted by the former British Educational Communications and Technology Agency (BECTA, 2007), the lead agency in the United Kingdom for the promotion and integration of information and communications technology until 2011, when funding was no longer available. BECTA researchers found more positive results for interactive whiteboard use in the primary grades than they did for IWB use in upper grades. One conclusion was a positive correlation between the length of time students interacted with each other on the whiteboard and higher national test scores. Literacy, math, and science learning made measurable gains with interactive whiteboard use, some showing as much as five months of additional progress. Overall enthusiasm for learning was noticed and attributed to students being able to see lessons better, being able to access materials through touch, and being exposed to an increased variety of lessons that the IWB enabled.

If the interactive whiteboard is used only as a marker board, then no more difference in student achievement will be noticed than if someone were using the chalkboard, overhead projector, or chart paper. Using the interactive whiteboard only as a basic display of information is like using a Ferrari only to drive down the street to get groceries.

Teachers who use the interactive whiteboard to demonstrate difficult concepts use the board to convey a process and use the software's functionality to the fullest extent. They take learning far beyond what a simple display board ever could.

Involving students in the process is crucial to attentive learning. The interactive whiteboard must be touched by students. In fact, highly successful learning groups often have students lead the discussions at the board or in small groups at learning centers or stations. Students should be active participants in their education and take ownership of the process.

When planning lessons that use the interactive whiteboard in order to increase student achievement, the teachers' focus should be on the substance of the content and not on the flashiness of the features. Local, state, and national education standards—some of which are noted later in this book—need to be addressed, and short-term objectives and long-term goals should be identified. Planning for differentiated learning within lessons will help meet the needs of all learners and keep the reason for the lessons in the forefront. These principles are not technology-specific, but they contain good practice measures to consider when implementing board-based lessons.

Due to students' excitement about using the IWB, some teachers have noticed increased student attendance. Increased student attendance equates to more instructional time, and more quality instructional time can increase achievement. Using this multi-faceted, multisensory tool makes the instruction time more engaging. But more school time by itself does not mean more achievement; a better use of time is what increases learning.

A good teacher with the right tools, such as an interactive whiteboard, creates the best conditions for measurable learning.

Student Motivation

Children are multitasking at younger ages. Their personal lives can include playing on a tablet while having the television on while talking to their parents, all simultaneously. Their behaviors and expectations are developing differently from previous generations. One toy, one purpose, one focus may have been what we took for granted growing up, but today's students expect multiple inputs and the ability to control their devices' functions.

You may have to reach outside your comfort zone to do so, but providing interactive learning experiences with two-way conversations, discussions that include explanations and reasoning, demonstrations of concepts, and opportunities to touch an interactive whiteboard motivates students to learn in ways that they understand. Higher motivation leads to greater participation. An active, engaged learning style matches the needs of our current generation of students, who are accustomed to being active participants in whatever they do. Part of our job is to develop lifelong learners. We need to adapt to their means of learning so they enjoy learning.

Finding what motivates students to learn has always been a challenge. Younger children are typically a little easier to motivate than older ones. In our favor, younger students have to a lesser degree the self-esteem issues or peer-influence struggles that their peers in the upper grades have. Younger students are typically still focused on making the teacher happy and getting good grades for themselves and their parents. But for more difficult subjects, such as speaking in front of the class, a dangled carrot may still be needed to encourage volunteers. An interactive whiteboard can be the carrot to get them involved.

Teachers may find that there is incredible power to motivate young students by making even minor changes in how a lesson is delivered, changes that are easily accomplished with an interactive whiteboard. For instance, for generations teachers have used the "A is for apple, B is for ball, C is for cat" system of pairing common words with letters of the alphabet. With most interactive whiteboard software, changing the content to the names of students present in the classroom, such as "A is for Ava, B is for Billy…" and having the students' faces replace the images of apples, balls, and cats can have a profound effect on a class by making the learning truly personal.

Alternately, you might find that some words aren't optimal or appropriate for your particular students. For instance, if you're teaching students in a remote Alaskan fishing village, you might substitute the word cod for cat. Perhaps your students speak Spanish as their first language, and the image of el gato next to a big C would confuse them. Substitution is easy with an IWB.

Using smilies, tallies, stars, picture stamps, or other creative ways to tie in the clip art or animated pictures from the software can serve as motivation for students to behave or to encourage them to reach a goal. For example, the collective class goal could be filling up a digital popcorn box that is displayed on the IWB. Pieces of popcorn could be earned by specific actions and then added to the box to reinforce positive group expectations. A filled popcorn box then equates to a real popcorn snack provided by the teacher. Symbolism to reflect real-life rewards can be used, depending on the graphics available.

Some software enables the user to change the writing tool's line pattern from a solid line to a dashed line, a sparkly line, or to a series of smilies. Changing the line pattern from boring solid black to something more exciting can encourage students to write on the board in front of the class. Writing in front of peers can be nerve wracking for students, but when getting a turn at the board becomes highly desirable, the task turns into a perceived reward rather than a negative social event.

Teacher Motivation

As with any other tool in a classroom, the power and effectiveness of an interactive whiteboard is primarily determined by how it is used by the teacher. The key to successful IWB use has very little to do with your brand of board or projector. A motivated teacher with even a basic interactive whiteboard is likely to be more successful than an indifferent educator with a complex IWB system brimming with state-of-the-art software and features.

How often teachers use the whiteboard, their attitudes toward it, and how much effort they expend to learn the system and software help determine how successfully they integrate the IWB with instruction. Therefore, lesson banks and training (sometimes free) are offered by vendors to ensure that you understand the positive results that can be achieved. Teacher involvement is just as important as student involvement. One involved teacher plus one involved class of students equals many parties who benefit.

The interactive whiteboard has been known to motivate teachers to enjoy teaching certain lessons again. We all have been there: The dreaded lesson comes up that we have to teach because it's important or mandated, yet it is difficult to teach because of content. But using an interactive whiteboard, with letters twirling, pictures flicking, and highlighting or spotlighting tools, can help to highlight areas in lessons and better explain content. An interactive whiteboard is like having a live graphic organizer. Organizing information in a visual manner can help students think in ways that help them better understand the curriculum. A teacher's love for teaching (or love for teaching certain lessons) can be reinvigorated when they are creating student-learning success in a fun atmosphere.

Meeting Technology Standards

The NETS•S (National Educational Technology Standards for Students) developed by the International Society for Technology in Education (ISTE) are recognized as the standards for skills that students need to succeed in our digital age. The interactive whiteboard helps provide opportunities to meet those standards. See the Appendix in this book for ISTE's NETS•S and NETS•T (National Educational Technology Standards for Teachers). Following is a brief overview of NETS•S concepts and how using an interactive whiteboard can help meet those standards.

Standard 1: Creativity and Innovation. This standard can be met thanks in part to the natural state of the board: a blank canvas. Digital content is created by students or by the teacher directed by the students. Drawings can be handmade and are limited only by artistic talent and imagination. Thoughts can be written or drawn out and categorized using a preexisting or original graphic organizer. Being able to write and draw creatively on top of any image or text makes the organization of knowledge open-ended and adaptable to a variety of learners. The blank canvas also makes brand-new ideas and innovations easier to conceive because of the open-ended organizational nature of the interactive whiteboard.

Standard 2: Communication and Collaboration. Meeting this standard is facilitated by best-practice interactive whiteboard use. This includes multiple students doing an activity together, such as playing a game or students working as a group to solve a teacher's puzzle. Students verbally interact with one another and also interact with the teacher. The board is not considered a personal device like a laptop or tablet. Different types of digital media created by others can be displayed through the whiteboard's projector and then marked up with the pen. Additionally, multimedia files can be created via the board software, so other students both locally and from a distance can learn a concept. The distant students can learn concepts on an interactive whiteboard in the same way that the local students did in the classroom.

Standard 3: Research and Information Fluency and **Standard 4: Critical Thinking, Problem Solving, and Decision Making.** Using an interactive whiteboard's ability to display collected information helps students meet these two standards by allowing them to organize the information in different ways and by helping them process what was discovered. Let's say that students, as a whole class or by group, are conducting research for a project. Once they have gathered information from multiple digital resources, that data needs to be displayed and organized. Using graphic organizers, collecting and displaying images, and drawing on charts can help students analyze what was found and help the group come to agreement on how to proceed with the project. In addition to collecting and holding the data, the final product or results can be shown using the interactive whiteboard. The end result may include various multimedia, both from other sources and from those originally created via the board software or the computer connected to the board.

Standard 5: Digital Citizenship. Digital citizenship is demonstrated by maintaining a positive attitude when using the interactive whiteboard technology. Students who enjoy using technology in school are developing healthy habits needed in a digital age. These students are developing a love for learning that they may not find when they use traditional paper resources. As information is gathered from digital sources to use with instruction, teachers who practice legal and ethical behaviors openly and honestly demonstrate for students how to be good digital citizens themselves.

Standard 6: Technology Operations and Concepts. This standard is met every time students touch the interactive whiteboard or technology connected to the board. In addition to just interacting with the whiteboard software, students should learn to use the software to accomplish other tasks. They should also be using nonboard software on the connected computer and displaying it through the interactive whiteboard. Learning all these different technologies will help students extend their current use of these tools. The knowledge will then transfer to new technology later, as students come into contact with it.

Although it is not the only way, the interactive whiteboard can be used as one means to meet some of the technology standards for students as set forth by ISTE. In combination with other technology experiences, the interactive whiteboard exposes students to digital tools that will help them adapt to new digital resources that have yet to be developed.

PART THREE

EXPLORE
LESSON IDEAS
AND RESOURCES

Transitioning Lessons to the IWB

Teachers new to using their interactive whiteboards may want to start by transferring teaching styles and familiar activities to the IWB. Teaching methods that you are already using, such as sportscaster style (see below), may work well with the IWB. Writing and drawing activities are particularly suited to working on an IWB. Physical maps are easily replaced with online and up-to-date digital maps. Many web-based games, activities, and tools are suited to IWB use. If a task can be done on your computer, there is no reason it cannot be done on your interactive whiteboard.

Sportscaster-Style Teaching

Writing or drawing on top of an image or text is easy to do with an interactive whiteboard. This is what is known as *sportscaster-style* teaching. Sportscasters on television review plays by drawing lines and arrows over the actual picture of the players on the field. Sportscaster-style teaching allows for a visual representation of what is being verbally explained.

Many teachers naturally use the sportscaster style of teaching without even realizing it. They circle and underline words on the chalkboard or marker board to draw attention to the words. They draw arrows to point out something relevant. Using overhead projectors, teachers use different-colored markers to identify different areas of content, such as parts of a sentence. Sometimes a black marker is used to simply fill in the blanks.

Similarly, the IWB can be used to give interactive properties to a traditional book. Writing on the board over the image of a book can help to point out different story parts, words, letters, characters, and main ideas. A book can be projected through a document camera or sometimes found online for free or through a subscription service. If the text is all that is sought, displaying an ebook will work. By marking up the book, using sportscaster style on the IWB, teachers can help students focus on the concepts being taught.

The same teaching tips that are employed when reading big books to young students can also be used when making an even bigger book by projecting it onto the whiteboard. Benefits for students include the teacher showing, by modeling and pointing, where students should focus while reading. Print concepts can be taught to beginning readers by the teacher interacting with the text. If students read together, they get to taste success by reading something that they are not able to read independently. Traditional print literature in big-book form can accomplish these tasks and others at a basic level. A digitized copy of the book or interactive book from a subscription service, coupled with the interactive capabilities of a board, can accomplish these tasks and others at a deeper level. An interactive whiteboard provides access to multitudes of colors instead of the basic ones, picture stamping in strategic areas, spotlight tools, zooming, shading tools to read one line at a time, saving the sportscaster markups for other uses, all allowing more ways for students and teachers to interact and extend learning.

Writing and Drawing Activities

If your interactive whiteboard reacts to any touch and not just to the pen that accompanies it, then using pointer sticks normally reserved for big books spices up using the board even further. Students' excitement about choosing a sword or animal-tipped stick makes taking turns even more special. Soft balls can add a bit of excitement by tossing them lightly onto the surface of a touch-sensitive IWB. Games can be created that react when a bubble, a balloon, or other large-surfaced graphic gets hit by the soft ball. A fly swatter can be used to gently swat letters, words, shapes, or numbers. Add a bug drawing or a picture behind the letters or shapes, and the realism of swatting a bug is generated. The more fun a tool is for students to use, the more excitement surrounds taking a turn.

If the interactive whiteboard necessitates using a particular pen, then putting the emphasis on the pen can generate the same effect as a different type of touch device. Creating names, such as *magic pen*, *doodle drawer*, or *magic marker*, will make holding the pen seem more special to a student. It's all in how you present it!

Many types of interactive whiteboard software enable a user to change pen color and line style. Some software even leaves a trail of pictures as a line is drawn. Color should be used with a purpose, such as identifying letters and numbers, vowels and constants, or nouns and verbs. Color and style act as an accent to emphasize a point; if these features are used for anything beyond emphasizing a point, then they detract from the message. Compare this to a computer-assisted presentation you may have seen in which the speaker overused animations, transitions, sounds, color, or clip art. The message can be lost in the decorative splash.

Simple erasing can also be used on the IWB as a tool for learning. Hide-and-seek type learning games can be played using the eraser. For example, students may close their eyes while a teacher erases selected content on the board, and then upon opening their eyes, students guess what is missing. The teacher may also erase content to make a point, such as erasing parts of a sentence to discuss how one word can change the meaning of a sentence. Using the eraser to reveal an answer can also be a great use of this standard software tool. Many interactive whiteboards include a "spotlight" feature that allows you to digitally cover the screen and move a spotlight over the screen to reveal what is underneath.

Most IWB-specific software includes shape-drawing tools. Beyond their use for simple shape recognition, drawing shapes can help reinforce counting, arithmetic word problems, and any other instance in which a picture is needed but no picture or stamping tool is available. Shapes can also be used to create an informal graphic organizer if students need help understanding information. A fancy pre-created template is not needed if you have access to shape tools. Shapes could also be used to open up lessons on measurement by serving as nonstandard units of measurement. For example, if you draw and make copies of a cube, students can move these cubes to measure a line that they have drawn ("the line is 5 cubes long").

Geography and Map Activities

Teaching geography and map skills can be accomplished through Google Maps, Google Earth, and any other online two- or three-dimensional map on an interactive whiteboard system. Once an interactive whiteboard is installed, physical maps in the classroom should come down; a physical map can show only a snapshot in time that is outdated by the time the map is mounted. The ability to move in any direction around the world easily, zoom in and out, measure distances with embedded tools, and get a sense for really being at a location through satellite imagery are all reasons why the updated web resources are better than the outdated paper map. Having a student spin the Earth with his or her hand using Google Earth on an interactive whiteboard can draw out the same emotions as when you or I spun a physical globe in classrooms of the past.

Web-Based Games and Activities

The games found on educational gaming websites that students enjoy can make great whole-group lessons for students. There are many appropriate and simple web-based games that take only a couple minutes or less to play. By projecting them and playing them as a whole group, those same short games become teachable moments. Examples of these games can be found on the PBS Kids site (www.pbskids.org/games). A quick game of Alpha Bricks or Sorting Box makes a fun teaching activity. There also are more difficult games that take longer to play that are well-suited to a computer lab environment, where activities are needed for an entire period.

Games on the IWB that allow students to play against each other and use virtual buzzers or any type of item that students can touch or tap are the most interesting. Putting two players in front of the board with the rest of the class watching can elicit cheering spectators and increase engagement for everyone.

The following is a list of sources for some free Flash, Shockwave, or Java-based games that generally are played by one or two students on a single computer—but can engage an entire classroom when the games are projected on an interactive whiteboard. There are many more games available on the web, and new ones are created daily, so consider this list simply as a place to start. These websites are cross-categorical gaming websites that appear in no particular order other than alphabetical. As with any web resource, the site manager is responsible for content, which may change over time. Please take precautions and preview all games ahead of time before using them with students.

ABCya
www.ABCya.com

This well-designed website goes beyond the ABCs. First, a teacher can select the grade level. Then, all the activities are broken out by subject areas. Like most of the free websites, ABCya.com is supported by advertising.

Arcademic Skill Builders
www.arcademicskillbuilders.com

Although there are some language arts, geography, and typing activities offered on this site, this website is primarily about math concepts. Activities can be easily sorted by grade level or subject. The website is free for the games, but if you want score tracking reports or customizable content, you will need to subscribe to Arcademics Plus for a small fee.

BBC Learning Schools
www.bbc.co.uk/schools

Games on this website can be sorted by age ranges. Some of the activities are suitable for students up through 16 years old. All activities are free. The website's offerings go beyond games to include instructional videos as well. Once you dig a little within the categories, you will find good activities to use with students.

Coolmath Games

www.coolmath-games.com

> Just as the name suggests, this free site is all about math games. Unique to this website are puzzles and board games that are ideal for projecting onto an interactive whiteboard. This website's design is a little congested, but the games are fun once you find the ones you want.

Count Us In

www.abc.net.au/countusin

> The basic activities from this site get right to the point: They are all designed around basic mathematics concepts. There is no advertising or cost, just very simple activities that get right to the skill. They are particularly good for very young students struggling with counting and numeric order.

Funbrain

www.funbrain.com

> Online games, books, and comics are included in this free resource from Pearson Education. The Funbrain games are developed for students through middle school. Math and literacy games are found by going to the "All Games" tab, which is categorized by grade levels. Included are some fun word-play games such as Mad Libs.

Funschool

http://funschool.kaboose.com

> Plenty of original free online games are found at this website. Clicking on "All Games" brings up a choice of subject areas, and clicking a subject shows you the list of games. Each game has an informative description so you know what it is about before entering it. There are many games to choose from.

GameGoo

www.earobics.com/gamegoo

> This free, professional website has a variety of literacy activities designed by the same company that developed the Earobics reading intervention program, a paid program for students who struggle with reading. The activities are categorized by difficulty level. Games are geared for Kindergarten through second grades.

ICT Games
www.ictgames.com/literacy.html

This site offers basic literacy and math activities that can help support your lessons. It also offers printables that extend the activities found on the site. Little to no customization is available. The cost is free, and the site is supported by advertising.

Illuminations
http://illuminations.nctm.org

This free website, sponsored by the National Council of Teachers of Mathematics (NCTM), provides more than one hundred online activities that are well designed, ready for interactive whiteboard use, and categorized by grade-level groups. All Illuminations activities are aligned with the Principles and Standards for School Mathematics.

Knowledge Adventure
www.knowledgeadventure.com

Many games and activities can be found on this free website, which can be searched by grade level, subject area, and age level (including activities for 4-year-olds). All games are geared toward Kindergarten through sixth grades.

Learning Games for Kids
www.learninggamesforkids.com

Health, geography, animals and nature, and hand-eye coordination games are among the many types included on this website. These are subjects that you do not always find on the web. Games are designed for pre-Kindergarten through fifth grades, and all games are free.

Mr. Nussbaum
http://mrnussbaum.com

Games found on this website are unique and cover a variety of different subject areas. The games are free, but if you want tracking, custom content, and custom settings, there is a cost. This is worth a look for some original games instead of the similar ones found on most sites.

PBS Kids Games

http://pbskids.org/games

These games include PBS's characters involved in many different early-learning activities. Although many are academic, some are more social in nature and include eating healthily and helping out. The website is free and includes many more games than other similar websites in this listing.

Play Kids Games

www.playkidsgames.com

This free website offers many games that teach general math and literacy skills as well as geography, art, and music. It also allows you to create a classroom area where you can upload your own content into their games. The activities are for the very young children through middle school ages.

Scholastic: Interactive Whiteboard Activities

http://teacher.scholastic.com/whiteboards

Scholastic has compiled some interactive whiteboard resources that are helpful to teachers, parents, and students alike. Activities are categorized by subject area, and each activity has associated whiteboard tips. The tips provide some directions specific to interactive whiteboard users. All activities are free, although additional shopping options are available.

School Time Games

www.schooltimegames.com

More than two hundred games are freely available on this website. The biggest attraction of this site is that it goes beyond math and literacy; it has many games to support science and social studies.

Sesame Street

www.sesamestreet.org/games

Although this website is slightly confusing to navigate, it offers a wealth of free educational games that include the familiar Sesame Street characters. Activities involve real kids explaining what to do, along with the animated characters, helping to maintain interest and attention. Games can be chosen by topic and age range.

Sheppard Software

www.sheppardsoftware.com

> These educational games are designed with many sounds and colors and with multilevels of difficulty. Games are categorized by subject and grade level. The website is free, and a version without advertising is available for a cost. Effective activities with good use of multimedia to accentuate skills are highlighted in these lessons.

Starfall

www.starfall.com

> The primary-level content on this site focuses on the big five areas of literacy: phonemic awareness, phonics, vocabulary, fluency, and comprehension. The activities are listed by specific skill. This website displays beautifully on a large space because of its simple and clean design. More content is available for a fee.

Web 2.0 Tools for Interactive Whiteboards

Interactive presentations, productivity, communication, and multimedia tools, otherwise known as Web 2.0, can take full advantage of an interactive whiteboard. The following are just a few of those that can be adapted to classroom curricula.

Animoto

http://animoto.com

> Animoto is a video creation service that that makes it possible for anyone to compile photos, videos, and music into a video, offering the means to teach through multimedia.

Befuddlr

http://befuddlr.com

> Using images from Flickr, Befuddlr turns photos into scrambled picture puzzles for users to solve.

bubbl.us

www.bubbl.us

> This service gives users a virtual whiteboard space to capture brainstorming ideas into a visual format that can be printed or exported.

Glogster
http://edu.glogster.com
> Users can create online multimedia posters to express ideas, thoughts, and feelings on any topic.

Join.me
https://join.me
> Join.me allows multiple classrooms to get on the same page—literally: It enables a teacher to create a screen-sharing session with another classroom. A free trial is available.

Masher
www.masher.com
> Users can combine their own content (video, music, and photos) to create presentations.

Prezi
http://prezi.com
> Prezi describes itself as a "presentation tool that helps you organize and present your ideas." Content can be presented in a nonlinear format by mapping ideas and topics rather than by using the traditional slide format.

Scriblink
http://scriblink.com
> This service offers a digital whiteboard that users can share online in real time.

Spell with Flickr
www.metaatem.net/words
> On this site, users type in a word, and the word is spelled out using images of letters from Flickr.

VoiceThread
http://voicethread.com
> VoiceThread can be used to create multimedia slideshows that others can comment on by multiple methods.

Wordle
www.wordle.net

> Words from user-provided text are organized in graphically formatted "word clouds" that give visual prominence to words that are used most often.

Helpful Teacher Tools

There are ample low- or no-cost productivity websites that are helpful for teachers. The following websites are more teacher-centered rather than student-centered, although some lend themselves well to whiteboard lessons.

Armored Penguin
www.armoredpenguin.com/crossword

> Teachers can create their own simple crossword puzzles using this crossword puzzle maker.

Assign-A-Day
http://assignaday.4teachers.org

> This site allows teachers to create calendars to manage classes and assignments.

Create a Graph
http://nces.ed.gov/nceskids/createagraph

> Teachers can use this site to make a variety of charts or graphs, including line and bar graphs and pie charts. This site is run by the National Center for Education Statistics.

Flashcard Exchange
www.flashcardexchange.com

> Flashcard Exchange allows users to use flashcards created by others and to create, share, export, and print their own flashcards.

FunnelBrain
www.funnelbrain.com

> Flashcards can be made collaboratively by groups of students. The flashcards support photos, video, and audio.

Google Docs
http://docs.google.com
> This suite of online tools allows teachers to create and share online documents, spreadsheets, and presentations.

Pixlr
http://pixlr.com
> Pixlr is an online photo editor that allows users to crop and resize photos, fix flaws, and apply effects.

PodOmatic
www.podomatic.com
> PodOmatic features podcast listings and a place to post podcasts.

Puzzlemaker
www.discoveryeducation.com/free-puzzlemaker
> Users can use this site to create a variety of puzzles, including word searches, simple crosswords, and math squares.

RubiStar
http://rubistar.4teachers.org
> Teachers can create rubrics online to teach as well as to evaluate learning projects.

ScreenCastle
www.screencastle.com
> ScreenCastle features screencast recording software that users can use to record from their browsers.

SlideShare
www.slideshare.net
> Users can create sharable presentations that can be made available to anyone.

TeacherLED
www.teacherled.com
> This site is focused on interactive whiteboard resources. Teachers can find Flash-based tools to maximize use of any type of interactive whiteboard.

TeacherTube

http://teachertube.com

TeacherTube is home to educationally relevant videos, photos, audio files, and documents.

Wordsmith

www.wordsmith.org/anagram

This simple tool creates anagrams from text entered by users (limited to 15 letters).

xtimeline

www.xtimeline.com

Teachers can create web-based timelines here that include pictures and videos. Timelines can be shared on the site.

Zoho Applications

www.zoho.com

This online suite offers word processing, spreadsheet, and presentation applications, as well file sharing and task management capabilities.

SurveyMonkey

www.surveymonkey.com

SurveyMonkey has software for creating online surveys and polls with immediate feedback.

Lesson Sparks

The following section contains IWB lesson ideas that meet specific Common Core State Standards. These are not full lesson plans. One-size lesson planning never fits all, and as educators, we constantly adapt lesson plans to fit our unique needs. These "lesson sparks" are intended to spark your imagination on how to use your interactive whiteboard in your environment. The lesson sparks are listed by category, and following each spark is the related Common Core State Standard (www.corestandards.org).

Language Arts

 Using graphics or handwritten letters, place all 26 letters of the alphabet independently and randomly on the board. Make sure that they are moveable and not locked in one spot. Have the students, as a whole class or in small groups, organize the letters in alphabetical order. Do this more than once by starting with the letters mixed up differently. One time all lowercase letters can be used, and another time all uppercase letters could be used, or any combination thereof.

Reading: Foundational Skills—Print Concepts

RF.K.1 Demonstrate understanding of the organization and basic features of print.

 Your interactive board software may have a template for a matching game with cards that you can customize. If it does not, several websites offer free and fee-based customizable content. Customize the cards so that there is an uppercase and lowercase letter to match for each letter. Students play the game by coming up to the board to touch two cards per turn to see if they select an uppercase and lowercase match. This game does not have to be played in pairs; it is equally fun to play as a whole group. It can be played keeping point totals, trying to beat a time using a clock, or just for fun.

Reading: Foundational Skills—Print Concepts

RF.K.1 Demonstrate understanding of the organization and basic features of print.

Place 26 or fewer simple words on the board. Each word should begin with a different letter of the alphabet. Students alphabetize the list by moving the words around. The activity can be made more complex by having multiple words with the same initial letter and increasing how many letters in the word need to be looked at to alphabetize the list correctly.

Reading: Foundational Skills—Print Concepts

RF.K.1 Demonstrate understanding of the organization and basic features of print.

Use sorting circles, a chart, or a pre-created sorting template from your software to sort out words that begin with a specific sound from ones that do not. Fill the bottom of your board with clip art or stamps. Make sure a large portion of the objects begin with the sound of the lesson focus. Have the students take turns dragging the pictures to the correct place on the board.

Reading: Foundational Skills—Phonological Awareness

RF.K.2 Demonstrate understanding of spoken words, syllables, and sounds (phonemes).

Using clip art or online graphics, place pictures randomly around the board. Some should begin with the target sound being taught, and others should not. Ask students to draw an X on top of the ones that do not begin with the sound. They can circle or put a checkmark next to the ones that do. This activity can be done using middle and ending sounds as well.

Reading: Foundational Skills—Phonological Awareness

RF.K.2 Demonstrate understanding of spoken words, syllables, and sounds (phonemes).

Using online graphics, clip art, or stamps in the software, create multiple pairs of pictures that when said aloud rhyme. Mix the pictures on the screen. Have students find the matching rhyming pictures and move the pair to another part of the screen. This can be made slightly more challenging by having groups of three or four rhyming pictures.

Reading: Foundational Skills—Phonological Awareness

RF.K.2 Demonstrate understanding of spoken words, syllables, and sounds (phonemes).

Students can drag word-family letters to match pictures that have the beginning letter next to each one. For example, add to the board a picture of a dog. Next to it should be the letter d. On the bottom of the board should be the grouped letters og. Load the board with a handful of pictures with the same word family to reinforce the concept. Students take turns moving the word-family letters to complete the words. One possible adaption can be using multiple word families at the same time on the board to drag to the corresponding pictures.

Reading: Foundational Skills—Phonics and Word Recognition

RF.K.3 Know and apply grade-level phonics and word analysis skills in decoding words.

Focus the lesson on one word family. Write as many words as you wish from that family on the board. Then write those words on the board again with a letter missing from each one of them. The missing letter could be any part of the word: front, middle, or end. Place the missing letters independently somewhere else on the board so they can be dragged over to complete the words. Students would drag the letters until they are used up, encouraging them to use strategy and to think ahead.

Reading: Foundational Skills—Phonics and Word Recognition

RF.K.3 Know and apply grade-level phonics and word analysis skills in decoding words.

 Use opposite colors when teaching onset-rime phonics; if your software allows layers, use those layers to hide one or the other. For example, let's take the word show. Imagine two large boxes that are layered behind the text. One is black, and the other is white. The background behind the two boxes is red. For the text colors, the sh in show is black and the ow in show is red. As the word show is slid atop the background, only the black sh shows because the ow in red matches the background color. As it moves across the black box, now the red ow shows but not the black sh. Dragging it farther to the white box will show the entire word. Using text and background color strategically will mimic a hiding effect and a magic reveal for students.

Reading: Foundational Skills—Phonics and Word Recognition

RF.K.3 Know and apply grade-level phonics and word analysis skills in decoding words.

A horizontal straight line can provide a good writing base for a handwriting lesson of a letter or number. Using two lines of different colors can help differentiate the top line from the bottom. Using a green dot where you start and a red dot where you stop provides a color cue to help students remember how the letter or number is formed.

Language—Conventions of Standard English

L.K.1 Demonstrate command of the conventions of standard English grammar and usage when writing or speaking.

Use lined paper graphics that match the same physical paper that students will write on. If no graphics are available in the software or online, you can scan lined paper. Display the scanned image through the interactive whiteboard, and write on top of it to demonstrate correct letter formation in relation to other letters. Using similar paper models, you can correct writing skills when students work independently.

Language—Conventions of Standard English

L.K.1 Demonstrate command of the conventions of standard English grammar and usage when writing or speaking.

Teaching students how to write a simple sentence can be done using puzzle pieces. Draw puzzle pieces or use software-generated puzzle pieces that fit together horizontally. Write one word on each puzzle piece, and mix up the puzzle pieces. Students should move the pieces around into the correct order and then read the sentence. The pieces should only fit together if the sentence is in the correct order.

Language—Conventions of Standard English

L.K.1 Demonstrate command of the conventions of standard English grammar and usage when writing or speaking.

Place a simple sentence on the board to teach verbs. The verb of the sentence can be left blank. The noun can also be left blank for fun. In playing this game, the noun should be decided at random by the teacher, a picture dice, or some other method. For example, the format of the sentence could be "The _____ can _____." Once the noun is chosen, the student gets to fill in the verb for fun in the same way that Mad Libs are played.

Language Standards—Conventions of Standard English

L.K.1 Demonstrate command of the conventions of standard English grammar and usage when writing or speaking.

 If your software has a dice graphic that allows it, add a letter to each side of the dice. The letters should be a mix of vowels and consonants found frequently in words. Place the dice side-by-side on your display to form a word. To start off easy, begin with three dice, with the first and third full of consonants and the middle one containing vowels only. Students should tap the dice for the dice to spin and land on a randomly selected letter. Have students read the entire word aloud and determine if it is a nonsense word or not. A student or teacher can write the randomly generated words on the bottom in T-chart form. One side is for nonsense words and the other for real words.

Reading: Foundational Skills—Phonics and Word Recognition

RF.1.3 Know and apply grade-level phonics and word analysis skills in decoding words.

Show a picture that has great detail and is of great interest to students. It can be one taken with a camera or one found on the web. Ask students to generate a list of adjectives to describe what they see. Students can write the list below the picture on the board.

Language—Conventions of Standard English

L.1.1 Demonstrate command of the conventions of standard English grammar and usage when writing or speaking.

 To help students learn about nouns, place circles, squares, or a pre-created chart on the board and write "person, place, or thing" next to each one of the areas. Place clip art of nouns on the board. Have students drag the clip art to the correct area that describes that type of noun.

Language—Conventions of Standard English

L.1.1 Demonstrate command of the conventions of standard English grammar and usage when writing or speaking.

 Sentence starters for emerging writers can help a student with writer's block. Display a graphic of an animal, a location, or a toy that would provide an idea or a topic to write about. On lined paper displayed on the board, start off with "I like ＿＿＿" or "I want ＿＿＿" to help them begin their sentences. Demonstrate letter formation, correct spacing, and how to write a complete sentence. After you have modeled proper writing, have the students take turns writing on the board prior to writing independently at their own desks.

Language—Conventions of Standard English

L.1.1 Demonstrate command of the conventions of standard English grammar and usage when writing or speaking.

Nouns and pronouns can be matched on the board. In a column on one side of the board, list some nouns. In a column on the other side of the board, list corresponding pronouns. Students can draw lines using their finger or pen, connecting nouns to their matching pronouns. Discuss why they match.

Language—Conventions of Standard English

L.1.1 Demonstrate command of the conventions of standard English grammar and usage when writing or speaking.

 Use two separated circles, squares, or a chart that will allow students to sort a predetermined set of words. For instance, perhaps the goal is to differentiate between adjectives and verbs. A student would click and drag the word *big* onto the side of the board that represents adjectives. Sorting the words would continue until all words in the pile are placed. This activity will work for all the different parts of speech or even for different intensities of verbs or adjectives.

Language—Conventions of Standard English

L.1.1 Demonstrate command of the conventions of standard English grammar and usage when writing or speaking.

 This next idea involves taking Daily Oral Language (DOL) and digitizing it. For example, if you are working on capital letters, you would write a sentence with missing capital letters. If your software has arrow graphics, have students drag the arrows underneath the letters where a capital letter should go. If no arrow graphics exist, students could circle or underline the letter or change the letter with an on-screen keyboard to correct the mistakes.

Language—Conventions of Standard English

L.2.2 Demonstrate command of the conventions of standard English capitalization, punctuation, and spelling when writing.

For teaching the differences between ending punctuation marks and when to use them, place a few simple sentences on the board and use color and grouping/ordering to provide a hide-and-reveal effect. Make the background color of the board white. Write the sentences in black text. The punctuation at the end should be written in the same color as the background (white, in this case), making it appear invisible. If your software allows it, group the elements and order the graphic to have it under the writing. The writing should be on top. Use a color-filled circle or a graphic, such as a magnifying glass with a color center, to reveal the punctuation by moving it under the punctuation mark. If your software does not allow grouping/ordering, use the cursor to highlight the punctuation mark, or change the color or the mark to reveal the answer. Have students guess the punctuation mark prior to the reveal of the correct answer.

Language—Conventions of Standard English

L.2.2 Demonstrate command of the conventions of standard English capitalization, punctuation, and spelling when writing.

 An electronic word-wall "dictionary" can be created on one whiteboard page for younger grades or on 26 linked pages for older students. On the page for younger learners, words can be added next to the appropriate letters to create a mini dictionary. In the case of the 26 linked pages, students would add words themselves to the corresponding pages. This interactive word wall, which mimics a dictionary, could be opened and available during writing times. The teacher can help by adding words to it. The entire page or file can be posted electronically and printed to be displayed.

Language—Conventions of Standard English

L.2.2 Demonstrate command of the conventions of standard English capitalization, punctuation, and spelling when writing.

Some students have difficulty organizing and writing paragraphs. Using the interactive whiteboard and graphics to visually organize the sentences can help students form coherent paragraphs. For example, you could have a sandwich graphic on the board large enough to allow students to write their sentences directly onto it. Explain that the layers represent the different sentences in a paragraph, with the top half of a bun being the introductory sentence, the bottom half being the conclusion, and the meat, cheese, and tomato in the middle being the supporting sentences. The same can be done with a large handprint graphic, writing on each of the five fingers.

Writing—Text Types and Purposes

W.3.2 Write informative/explanatory texts to examine a topic and convey ideas and information clearly.

Mathematics

 Interactive charts for working with mathematical "hundreds" can be found on the web and in some software packages. Students touch the number on the whiteboard while they count by means of ones, twos, fives, or tens. Some of the numbers spin when touched, while others change colors. Having the numbers react to touch draws interest in learning to count.

Counting and Cardinality—Know number names and the count sequence.

K.CC.1 Count to 100 by ones and by tens.

 To help teach number sequence, write a number on the interactive whiteboard followed (or preceded) by a blank line and then the answer. Cover the answer with a themed graphic or a box. Students come up to the board and on the blank line write the number that comes next/before. They can then move the graphic or box to see if their answer is correct. This game can also be used as a skip counting exercise.

Counting and Cardinality—Know number names and the count sequence.

K.CC.2 Count forward beginning from a given number within the known sequence (instead of having to begin at 1).

Counting buckets can be used to hold the number of items represented on the bucket. For example, line the bottom of the interactive whiteboard with baskets or buckets labeled with numbers. Fill the rest of the board space with an apple tree covered with apple graphics or red-filled circles. Students drag the apples from the tree into each bucket until the quantity matches the number written on the bucket.

Counting and Cardinality—Know number names and the count sequence.

K.CC.3 Write numbers from 0 to 20. Represent a number of objects with a written numeral 0–20 (with 0 representing a count of no objects).

Students can match number words with their corresponding numerals. Write the number words on one side of the board and spread out the numerals on the other side. Students then move the number words next to the matching numerals. To make further connections, they can draw dots next to the numerals or words to represent the amount.

Counting and Cardinality—Count to tell the number of objects.

K.CC.4 Understand the relationship between numbers and quantities; connect counting to cardinality.

Students can learn to sequence the order of events on the IWB while using the ordinal number language. Find or create pictures showing a sequence of events, for example, someone getting her coat, putting it on, and zipping it up. Display these pictures on the board and have students put them in the correct order while saying the appropriate terminology. Further ideas for picture sequences are what to do when students first come to school and how to solve a math problem.

Counting and Cardinality—Count to tell the number of objects.

K.CC.4 Understand the relationship between numbers and quantities; connect counting to cardinality.

 List the numbers one to five on the board. Next to them, draw blank lines representing the quantity of the number. For example, next to the number three you would draw three blank lines. Make available a number of squares or other themed graphics. Have students drag the graphics on top of the blank lines. This activity helps students quantify the meanings of those numbers.

Counting and Cardinality—Count to tell the number of objects.

K.CC.5 Count to answer "how many?" questions about as many as 20 things arranged in a line, a rectangular array, or a circle, or as many as 10 things in a scattered configuration; given a number from 1–20, count out that many objects.

 Place or draw a ten frame onto the interactive whiteboard to teach students the relationship between a number and quantity it represents. Ten frame graphics are available in some software packages and on the web. The frame can be filled to represent different amounts. Write a number on the board, and ask students to fill in the frame either by coloring the frame or by dragging graphics on top to match the number.

Counting and Cardinality—Count to tell the number of objects.

K.CC.5 Count to answer "how many?" questions about as many as 20 things arranged in a line, a rectangular array, or a circle, or as many as 10 things in a scattered configuration; given a number from 1–20, count out that many objects.

 Students can draw "greater than," "equal to," and "less than" symbols on the board to compare two sets of numbers. Put a graphic of a football field, basketball court, or a soccer field on the board and then write fictitious scores on either side of the field to represent different teams. Ask students to come up to the board and draw the correct symbol to compare the scores. Connecting the concept to a game scenario helps retain interest and demonstrate application of the terms.

Counting and Cardinality—Compare numbers.

K.CC.6 Identify whether the number of objects in one group is greater than, less than, or equal to the number of objects in another group, for example, by using matching and counting strategies.

 Students can solve simple story problems using graphics or shapes. For example, a teacher could draw a handful of filled circles inside a gumball machine graphic. The teacher could describe the following story problem to the students: Two yellow gumballs were bought by Sally. Three red gumballs were bought by Peter. How many gumballs were bought altogether? Students could touch and move the gumballs together to help solve the problem. This word problem could be adjusted as needed by filling in the circles with different colors and using different numbers of circles.

Operations and Algebraic Thinking—Understand addition as putting together and adding to, and understand subtraction as taking apart and taking from.

K.OA.2 Solve addition and subtraction word problems, and add and subtract within 10, for example, by using objects or drawings to represent the problem.

 Use graphics or the square shape on the board to represent connecting cubes. Write a number problem on the board. Have students connect cubes to represent each number in the equation, with each group of cubes a different color, then connect the groups to get a total. For example, 5 blue blocks connected to 5 red blocks equal 10 blocks total. Subtraction can also be taught by taking away from groups of connected blocks.

Operations and Algebraic Thinking—Understand addition as putting together and adding to, and understand subtraction as taking apart and taking from.

K.OA.2 Solve addition and subtraction word problems, and add and subtract within 10, for example, by using objects or drawings to represent the problem.

 Fill the interactive whiteboard with empty shapes of all sizes. Explain to students what color should be used to fill in each shape; for example, color all the squares orange. Students can use a pen or a fill tool to find and color all the shapes per the specified directions.

Geometry—Identify and describe shapes (squares, circles, triangles, rectangles, hexagons, cubes, cones, cylinders, and spheres).

K.G.2 Correctly name shapes regardless of their orientations or overall size.

Calendar time lends itself well to teaching mathematical concepts. Place a blank calendar on the interactive whiteboard. For every day that goes by, fill in the day with a shape that follows a pattern. Every calendar time, ask students to guess what shape comes next in the pattern and draw it in the space. To embed real-life shapes within the pattern, consider using digital photos of real objects to represent the shapes. For instance, a tile, window, markerboard or brick could all be used instead of a drawn rectangle.

Geometry—Identify and describe shapes (squares, circles, triangles, rectangles, hexagons, cubes, cones, cylinders, and spheres).

K.G.2 Correctly name shapes regardless of their orientations or overall size.

 Have the students draw shapes to match a shape that is already shown on the IWB. For example, place a picture of a triangle on the board and ask students to draw the same shape next to it. While this is taking place, use terminology such as "straight sides" or "pointy corners" to help students draw correctly and identify the differences between a triangle and other shapes.

Geometry—Analyze, compare, create, and compose shapes.

K.G.4 Analyze and compare two- and three-dimensional shapes, in different sizes and orientations, using informal language to describe their similarities, differences, parts (e.g., number of sides and vertices/"corners") and other attributes (e.g., having sides of equal length).

Have students complete picture puzzles (tangrams). Using the shape tools, draw a variety of empty shapes (outline only) and form them into a picture, or look online for pre-created tangram puzzles. Create filled versions of all the shapes in the picture and have these available on the sides of the board. Have students drag the filled shapes on top of the empty shapes that form the picture, continuing that process until all the spaces are filled in. Ask students to describe what types of shapes were used and how many. Math terminology, such as *rotation*, can be brought into the conversation, as the shapes will need to be adjusted to fit on top of the picture.

Geometry—Analyze, compare, create, and compose shapes.

K.G.4 Analyze and compare two- and three-dimensional shapes, in different sizes and orientations, using informal language to describe their similarities, differences, parts (e.g., number of sides and vertices/"corners") and other attributes (e.g., having sides of equal length).

 Using balloon graphics or balloons drawn on the board can help you teach subtraction. Write a subtraction problem using the quantities of balloons to represent the problem. Have students pop (or erase) the balloons to demonstrate the concept of take away. Popping-balloon graphics are found in some interactive whiteboard software and online. If you don't have them available, creating a popping sound as the student erases a balloon can be almost as fun.

Operations and Algebraic Thinking—Represent and solve problems involving addition and subtraction.

1.OA.1 Use addition and subtraction within 20 to solve word problems involving situations of adding to, taking from, putting together, taking apart, and comparing, with unknowns in all positions, for example, by using objects, drawings, and equations with a symbol for the unknown number to represent the problem.

Number problems with a missing number can be done in such a way as to reveal the answer once the equation is moved to another location on the board. Start by using a background color that matches the text color of the missing number. For example, assign a yellow background. Write the number sentence $1 + 4 = 5$, with the number 4 in the same color font as the background (yellow) and the rest of the equation in black. Place a large white rectangle on the bottom of the board. The equation can then be dragged down over the rectangle to show all of the colored text, revealing the unseen number. This process can be repeated with other number problems, whether addition or subtraction.

Operations and Algebraic Thinking—Represent and solve problems involving addition and subtraction.

1.OA.1 Use addition and subtraction within 20 to solve word problems involving situations of adding to, taking from, putting together, taking apart, and comparing, with unknowns in all positions, for example, by using objects, drawings, and equations with a symbol for the unknown number to represent the problem.

 Create nonstandard units of measurement with the shape tool, and use any graphic as the object to be measured. Start by creating a number of identically sized shapes, such as filled boxes, to use as measurement units and have them available to use at the bottom of the board. Put a graphic, a worm, for example, on the whiteboard and ask students to come up to the board and line up boxes underneath to show how many boxes long the worm is. You could add other graphics to the screen to use as comparisons.

Measurement and Data—Measure lengths indirectly and by iterating length units.

1.MD.1 Order three objects by length; compare the lengths of two objects indirectly by using a third object.

If your software allows flicking, your students can practice adding by using a dartboard graphic. To practice adding, place a graphic of a dartboard on the interactive whiteboard and use graphics of darts. Give each circular area on the dartboard a numerical value, just as there are on a physical dartboard. One student at a time should take a turn flicking the dart onto the dartboard. The students should total the points after a few flicks and write the answer.

Operations and Algebraic Thinking—Add and subtract within 20.

2.OA.2 Fluently add and subtract within 20 using mental strategies. By end of Grade 2, know from memory all sums of two one-digit numbers.

 Place value can be taught by using a chart that has a place for numbers to be written and a place where a box containing the correct value word can be dragged to match. For example, have a student write a number in the chart, such as 125. On the bottom of the whiteboard have three boxes: one with "hundreds" written in it, one with "tens," and one with "ones." After writing 125, the student would need to drag the correct box above the corresponding column in the chart.

Number and Operations in Base Ten—Understand place value.

2.NBT.1 Understand that the three digits of a three-digit number represent amounts of hundreds, tens, and ones; for example, 706 equals 7 hundreds, 0 tens, and 6 ones.

 Base-ten block graphics can be dragged to represent different numerical amounts. Place the base-ten blocks (ones, tens, hundreds) together on the board and write a number on the IWB. Have students drag the blocks they need to represent the number. Alternatively, you can drag the base-ten blocks to the board and have students write their correct numerical representations.

Number and Operations in Base Ten—Understand place value.

2.NBT.1 Understand that the three digits of a three-digit number represent amounts of hundreds, tens, and ones; for example, 706 equals 7 hundreds, 0 tens, and 6 ones.

Time can be compared digitally and in analog form (a clock with hands) to help student learn both. They both can be represented on the interactive whiteboard at the same time. Draw the hands on an analog clock and call up students to write the matching digital time on the board. The reverse could be done as well. The time could be random, or it could represent when the next transition will happen during the day, such as the end of the class period. Graphics and interactive timers are available through some software packages so that when one clock (analog or digital) is set, the other moves to match.

Measurement and Data—Work with time and money.

2.MD.7 Tell and write time from analog and digital clocks to the nearest five minutes, using a.m. and p.m.

Have the students count out coins to match a desired amount. Display graphics representing a mix of coin values and write an amount to be matched. Ask students to drag the coins as need to make the amount listed. For example, write 7¢ on the board. Students may drag seven pennies or one nickel and two pennies next to the 7¢. To make it more fun, display a graphic of a piggy bank or wallet for students to move the money into.

Measurement and Data—Work with time and money.

2.MD.8 Solve word problems involving dollar bills, quarters, dimes, nickels, and pennies, using dollar and cent symbols appropriately.

The concept of a pictograph is easy to demonstrate on an interactive whiteboard. User various, colorful graphics or stamps to graph anything from who had white or chocolate milk at lunch to who has birthdays during what month.

Measurement and Data—Represent and interpret data.

2.MD.10 Draw a picture graph and a bar graph (with single-unit scale) to represent a data set with up to four categories. Solve simple put-together, take-apart, and compare problems using information presented in a bar graph.

 Simple multiplication can be demonstrated by moving pictures into groups. For example, have six pictures available at the bottom of the screen, and draw two circles to represent two groups. Write the number sentence $2 \times 3 = 6$ on the board. Students can drag the pictures into the circles (three in each) to solve the problem and visualize its meaning.

Operations and Algebraic Thinking—Represent and solve problems involving multiplication and division.

3.OA.1 Interpret products of whole numbers, for example, interpret 5×7 as the total number of objects in 5 groups of 7 objects each. For example, describe a context in which a total number of objects can be expressed as 5×7.

 The concept of simple division can be explained by using sorting circles on the interactive whiteboard with the graphics of your choosing. Write a division problem on the board, and ask students to demonstrate what it means by using the correct number of sorting circles and dividing up the pictures into those circles. Using pictures of candy always seems to keep student interest!

Operations and Algebraic Thinking—Represent and solve problems involving multiplication and division.

3.OA.3 Use multiplication and division within 100 to solve word problems in situations involving equal groups, arrays, and measurement quantities, for example, by using drawings and equations with a symbol for the unknown number to represent the problem.

Science

 Conduct a color sort: Start by drawing two large empty shapes on the whiteboard. The shapes should be outlined with the two colors that you want to help students identify. Place the clip art or other graphics to be sorted along the bottom of the interactive whiteboard. For example, draw a large red-outlined square and a large yellow-outlined square on the board, and place graphics, such as a school bus, banana, sun, apple, barn, and tomato, at the bottom. Ask students to drag the pictures to the shapes to sort by appropriate color. The banana would be dragged to the large yellow-outlined square, the apple to the red-outlined square. Other sorting activities could be done by size or shape, with the sorting area outline mimicking the attribute being sorted.

 Talk about plant parts by drawing and labeling them. Have students draw the plant on the board, showing the different parts, or open a photo of the plant to use for the lesson. Then ask students to label the plant parts with their correct names. This same labeling activity can be done with parts of a bug, spider, or human body.

 Talk about the life cycle of an animal or plant using whiteboard graphics. This could be done with anything, such as a butterfly, an apple tree, or a pumpkin. Insert graphics on the whiteboard representing various points within the topic's life cycle. Have students move the pictures around the whiteboard into the correct order. Students can draw arrows between the pictures and should be encouraged to use ordinal numbers to help describe the order.

 The five senses can be taught using images on the interactive whiteboard. For example, you could put pictures of a chair and a skunk on the whiteboard and ask students which one you might know by using your sense of smell. Students could move pictures of eyes, ears, nose, tongue, and hands around the board next to other images to indicate the sense that best helps identify the object. For instance, putting a tongue next to an apple would represent that taste is a key sense used to identify the apple.

 Living and nonliving things can be displayed in the form of clip art for students to sort, identify, draw, cross out, or circle, depending on what is being identified. You can also have students drag the words "living" and "nonliving" next to pictures on the whiteboard to indicate the correct category.

 The concept of temperature can be taught by using a thermometer graphic commonly found in board software or by drawing your own thermometer. Students can adjust the red "mercury" level up or down. Start by displaying a picture, such as an ice cube, and have students match the mercury level to their estimation of the object's temperature. You could also say or write a temperature and ask for a student to draw a red line to match it. The concept being taught is identifying hot and cold objects, with red up high representing hot whereas red down low represents cold.

Our solar system can be taught in multiple ways using the interactive whiteboard. Display real pictures of the planets on the board and ask students to match the planet names to pictures. Students could also label the planets by writing on the board. Have students place the planets in order of distance from the sun on a picture of orbital tracks. Other ordering can be done according to the planets' gravitational pull or size.

 To teach about animal habitats, display photos of different habitats, and line the bottom of the interactive whiteboard with animal pictures. Have students drag the animals to match their appropriate habitats. If students are learning about one particular habitat, arrange of group of animal stamps on the board and have students, in groups, draw the habitat and its characteristics around the animals.

 To teach the concepts of day and night, place a picture of the Earth and a picture of the sun on the board. If the Earth graphic can be spun, that will help. Place the sun in the middle of the board. Move the Earth around the sun, and draw arrows to explain how it works. An adaption can be done to discuss seasonal temperature changes by adjusting the tilt of the Earth graphic.

 Reduce, Reuse, and Recycle differences can be taught by placing three recycling-bin graphics on the board. Make the bins different colors to help younger students differentiate among the three. Take different clip art and place it on the screen. Have students sort the clip art into the correct bin based on what they have learned about how to conserve Earth's resources.

Color mixing can be accomplished by creating shapes with primary colors and combining them. If your software allows it, make the shapes light enough to see through them. As you move your shapes on top of one another, students should see the same effects as if you were actually mixing colors together using paints on paper.

Demonstrating force and motion can be done if your board's software allows for flicking motion. Start with a large sports field graphic (e.g., football, soccer, baseball) labeled with numbers to represent distance. Pick a starting point on the field, such as the end zone of a football field, and have a graphic of the ball for students to move. Give students the opportunity to flick the ball across the field to see where it lands. You may want to bring the concept of estimation into the discussion by having students first mark where they think the object will land before they flick it. The same experiment can be done outside but with the equivalent physical object (football). Have students compare the estimates and the actual distance and discuss reasons for the differences between them, such as the force it would take to throw a ball a certain distance. These conversations may lead into reality/fantasy discussions about what is seen on electronic devices, games, television, and movies as opposed to the actual force (energy) it would take to move an object.

More Ideas

Discuss symmetry by drawing a line down the center of your whiteboard, either horizontally or vertically, depending on the types of graphics. Then put shapes or graphics of any kind on each side of the line. Both sides should have the same number, sizes, and shapes of graphics but placed in different locations on either side of the line. Have the students make the arrangement of shapes on one side symmetrical with the arrangement of shapes on the other side. A twist to this activity could be to take some graphics and place them over the line. Discuss which graphics are symmetrical versus which ones are not.

 Probability is a concept that can be explained through interactive graphics found on the web or in the whiteboard software, such as coins, dice, and spinners. Use coins that can be flipped or dice that spin and keep a tally of how they landed. Use spinners with different configurations to demonstrate different probabilities. For example, use a spinner divided into colors of equal areas and a spinner that has just a sliver of one color with the rest of the area in another color.

 Chronological timelines can be represented by a line and dates on the board. Find photographs or pictures appropriate to the topic and have them available on the board. Ask students to drag the pictures to the places where they belong on the timeline. For example, you may ask students to put presidents in order based on the years of their terms. Adding video or audio clips can help the timeline come to life.

 As a part of learning about patriotic symbols, students can assemble a country's flag, which helps them focus on the details of the flag. For example, if students are learning about the United States flag, draw an empty rectangle and have available a smaller blue rectangle, white and red stripes, and white stars. Have students drag the pieces into the correct places on the flag. Discuss the meaning of each piece as the flags are assembled.

Help students learn about emotions by using some type of dice, spinner, or other random generator. Assign a different emotion to each section or dice face. Have students roll or spin to land on a particular emotion and then describe a time when they felt that emotion. Discussion of the emotion can lead into descriptions of the emotion, using words and drawings and sharing ideas on how to cope with it.

 Activities that help students to identify their own and others' feelings and emotions can be supported by the whiteboard. Write several situations that evoke different feelings on the board and cover them up with a color boxes or balloons. Pick two students. Reveal a situation to the first student, making sure the rest of the class can't see what it is, then have the student act out that feeling. Have the second student guess the answer and then come up to the board to reveal, by lifting a shade or popping a balloon, whether the guess matched the emotion being acted out.

 Help students differentiate between what is a "need" versus what is just a "want" using the interactive whiteboard. Divide the board into two sides. One side of the board should reflect needs; you can prompt students by writing the words *food, clothing, shelter,* and *love* there. The side reflecting wants should be blank. Add clip art or web graphics for students to sort accordingly or have students write words for objects on the appropriate side.

 For encouraging dental health, you can display a mouth full of teeth and use a toothbrush graphic to demonstrate the proper way to brush by moving it in little circles. Color teeth with yellow and have the toothbrush act as an eraser to remove the color. Another idea for exploring dental health is sorting food by whether it is good for teeth or bad for teeth by moving specific types of food to "good" and "bad" sides of the whiteboard.

 A chart can be used to help the class take attendance without calling out names. Create a chart and have the words "At School" on one side and the words "At Home" on the other side. Start with a list of the names of everyone in class on the At Home side. As students arrive for the day, they should drag their names from the At Home side of the chart to the At School side. Write a mathematical word-problem representing the total number of students, students present, and students absent. The same type of chart can be used to determine who is receiving a school lunch as opposed to who brought lunch from home. This is also a good way to see who attended Open House or Curriculum Night.

 Exploring the calendar each morning can teach multiple skills. With a calendar on the interactive whiteboard, add the phrases "Yesterday was _____, today is _____, and tomorrow will be _____"—leaving spaces where students can drag and drop the corresponding days of the week. The calendar could include a list of months of the year, and students could move an arrow to point to the correct month. Ask students to use the pen or their finger to write out the day, month, and year in different formats (e.g., January 5, 2013 or 1/5/13). Students could record the weather for each day by adding appropriate graphics for sunny, partly sunny, cloudy, rainy, and snowy weather. Students could then use this data to create a weather bar graph with fillable boxes that represent how many days of each kind of weather were in the month thus far.

Game Templates

Television game shows can be turned into engaging IWB game templates that can hold whatever content is being taught. Using game templates can reduce the lesson creation time for teachers, as they can be used in multiple units of study. In addition to finding a pre-created template or using a self-created one, you may want to seek out websites, as previously mentioned in the book, for game programs that allow you to upload your own content.

These games should involve as much student movement and action as possible. For instance, if the class is playing a Family Feud-type game, have a podium or cart in front of the board so two students can stand up and tap their hands (or buzzers) in front of the class. The IWB will act as the answer board, and the teacher acts as the host. When it is time to check the answer, students can yell out "survey says" before the teacher reveals the answer.

Game shows will continue to be created beyond the writing of this book. The important point is to tap into popular culture and interest. The more current and popular the game or game show, and the more familiar the format, the more students will pay attention to the content. Heightened involvement and emotions can mean better memory and recall of the content.

The following list of game shows includes those that have been successfully adapted into games for the classroom.

Are You Smarter Than a 5th Grader?

Family Feud

Hollywood Squares

Jeopardy

Press Your Luck

Wheel of Fortune

Who Wants to Be a Millionaire?

Graphic Organizers

One of the strengths of an interactive whiteboard its facility to project images for the entire class to see and interact with. Using standard graphic organizers, such as a T-chart, flow chart, Venn diagram, or KWL chart ("What I know, what I want to know, what I learned"), can help students organize their thinking. Organized thinking helps students understand difficult concepts and ideas. Graphic organizers can also help prepare students to write cohesive paragraphs for a well-written, flowing story.

Beyond the basic graphic organizers, other imagery can be used to achieve the same goals. Think about how a simple image that is familiar to students, such as a flower with petals, can serve as a graphic organizer. The more interesting and familiar the image, the easier it may be for students to recall and keep that information organized. You could simply project the graphic organizer and allow students to write on it. Or if your software allows it, consider using a split screen. On one side place a paragraph or short story; on the other place the graphic organizer for students to use as they dissect the parts of the writing.

Graphically organizing thoughts and ideas on an interactive whiteboard can also extend learning beyond the board. Because it is digital, a page can be saved for later viewing, saved as a PDF for easy sharing, or printed on paper for students to hold in their hands. The printed version can be taken home, giving families the opportunity to reinforce lesson concepts at home. A digital file of the organizer could be posted on the web or emailed out to others. Students can use those images to remember what was taught. Digitizing learning material offers the huge advantage of broadening access to it.

Below is a nonexhaustive list of the types of graphics that you can develop to get started with using a graphic organizer. You do not need to be an artist to draw and take advantage of your own organizer.

cloud and raindrops

flower and petals

gears

pies

film strip

triangle up or down

magnifying glass

pillars on a building

outline of a person

hand(s)

Keep in mind that the interactive whiteboard community has been creating and sharing classroom-tested games, graphic organizers, and other content for years. Much of it is available for free. There are many reasons to create your own custom materials, but that doesn't mean that you need to create everything or that you can't use already existing ideas as the basis to start creating your own. It is very important, however, to honor software registration requirements, where appropriate, and to honor and respect both copyrights and online guidelines for online community sharing of these various games, graphic organizers, and content.

Using the Support Base

Teachers looking for interactive whiteboard support will find plenty of resources on the web. Teachers with interactive whiteboards have always supported one another, and websites are filled with shared lessons and ideas on how to use IWBs in teaching. Some of the sites are company sponsored and support teachers by hosting lesson banks, forums, and user communities; many offer resources such as tutorials, webinars, and white papers. The best thing about most of the lessons found on these websites is that they are teacher created, not company created. This is important because teachers are more likely know best what teachers need. The following are some sites where lessons and other resources can be found.

Hitachi CambridgeBoard/StarBoard Resource Centre
resourcecenter.hitachi-software.de

This United Kingdom-based, free resource center for StarBoards offers a no-frills approach for teachers who want to find or share activities. Content can be easily searched by grade and subject. Lessons are also available in several different languages. Although the content works only with Hitachi boards, the basic ideas can be adapted for other applications.

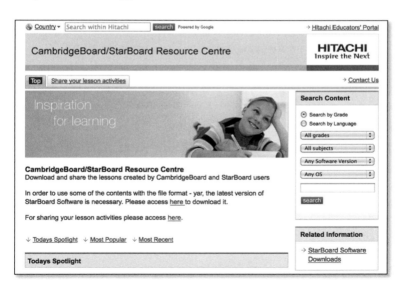

MimioConnect: Lessons and Activities
www.mimioconnect.com/lessons/all/all/all/new

The MimioConnect website offers an activity bank of lessons submitted by teachers all over the world. Activities can be sorted by date posted, rating, number of views, and contributor. They can also be filtered by subject and by grade level/age. Lessons are available in several different languages. Access to the site is free.

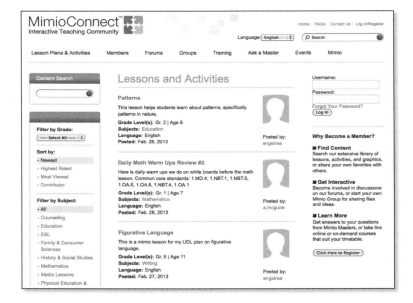

PolyVision Resources

www.polyvision.com/resources

PolyVision doesn't offer lessons but has a deep community of educators involved in blogs, Nings, and other sharing platforms. The resources on the site include webinars, white papers, video tutorials, case studies, and information on interactive whiteboard funding.

Promethean Planet

www.prometheanplanet.com

On the on Promethean Planet website, activities are free to download and can be searched by using multiple criteria. Although the lessons are proprietary to Promethean-brand products, the ideas can be transferred to other types of interactive whiteboards as well. Each lesson includes a preview so that teachers can see a quick view of the content before downloading.

SMART Exchange
http://exchange.smarttech.com

SMART Exchange categorizes activities by subject, grade, and file type. Although the downloadable activities are proprietary to SMART Board-brand products, the ideas themselves can be transferred to other types of interactive whiteboards. This is a free resource but does require registration to download, as do many of the sites listed in this category.

This is only a sampling of the many, many interactive whiteboard sites available for teachers wishing to share and gain knowledge from their peers. A huge number of educator blogs online don't necessarily deal exclusively with interactive whiteboards but may contain some valuable tips and resources for IWB use.

Building Support

Some teachers have not yet been convinced that an interactive whiteboard can transform learning. Disenchantment can often be traced back to how the board ended up in the classroom in the first place—almost always, decisions on big-ticket items, such as interactive whiteboards, are made at the building or district level. Unilateral decision making on how to spend large amounts of money can leave teachers feeling as if their input does not matter. In these situations, teachers must move beyond any initial resentment about how the interactive whiteboard arrived and shift their energy to discover how it can best be used in their classrooms. Teachers will also need to invest time and energy into finding training and resource materials to learn how to maximize effective use of the whiteboard.

The largest mistake a school or district can make is not having enough (or any) internal support to help teachers learn these new skills. Many times, grants or other large funding sources only take care of the equipment. Money to supply training, conferences, workshops, external site visits to other schools, and long-term internal support for using the technology is not available. At a bare minimum, an energetic and experienced cheerleader of interactive whiteboard use who represents your school should be sent to trainings with the understanding it is her or his job to support peers when asked. This cheerleader might be a technology facilitator, library media specialist, or technology integration specialist. If no such positions exist in your school, propose one to a budget manager in terms of dollars and cents. That budget manager could be a building administrator, department head, or superintendent. Propose a full-time, part-time, or stipend position to help protect the technology investment and its advancement. Using small amounts of district funds for such a purpose can help ensure that the large funding source is utilized fully and that its continued use can be justified.

Better teacher support results when that energetic cheerleader returns to focus on subject-specific training in partnership with content-specific coaches, such as math and literacy teachers or other subject specialists, to develop high-quality lessons. When instructional support is bundled with quality, plentiful technical support, and an adequate budget for technicians and maintenance, the basics are covered to support the investment in interactive whiteboards. If you have a district or school technology committee, make sure to join such a group and express your thoughts and support. For any successful technology initiative, planning and preparation are essential. Understanding and supporting the total cost of technology "ownership" is critical for success.

Having the support of educational administrators is key for teachers learning to integrate the interactive whiteboard into regular classroom use. Using the IWB in the most effective ways requires some experimental teaching methods. For some administrators—those who may view traditional note taking, choral reading, or worksheet use as preferable teaching methods—this experimental IWB learning curve is outside their comfort zone or the ways in which they were trained. To the untrained administrative eye, throwing a soft ball against a board, allowing students to lead a lesson, or engaging in interactive games may look like a teacher is not running the classroom. You may simply need to remind your administrators that you and other teachers need help and resources to make the best use of the investment. You may also need to remind them that effective uses of interactive technology will probably result in classrooms where students are noisier, more active, and more engaged—thus learning more effectively.

The relationship between teachers and the families of their students is also important. Just as you may be new to technology in your elementary classroom, so are the parents. Some parents see such technology as an amazing addition and wish they had had access to it while growing up. Others view most technology as unnecessary and question the cost relative to the benefits.

Being able to articulate the benefits of your interactive whiteboard to parents, as well as to administrators, can be beneficial for continuing the process of installing more interactive whiteboards and other classroom-based technology. Families can influence decisions by way of PTO and PTA meetings, committee meetings, and connections to the school board. It is tremendously helpful for families to know the value of interactive whiteboards in the classroom so they can support the use of this and other educational technology advancements.

CONCLUSION

If interactive whiteboards are used often and in depth, there should be little doubt that they can change the ways entire classrooms of students learn and remember. Interactive whiteboards have the ability to motivate students and get them involved in learning. Excited students who actively take a role in the learning process are more likely to do well with learning content.

A lot has been said about the place of tablets, such as the iPad and Android devices, in education. Some organizations have devoted resources to purchasing them solely due to the buzz and excitement surrounding tablets. Unfortunately, this effort is often made without enough thought given to consider best practices with the developmental needs of different-aged learners. Many times, younger students who are learning concepts for the first time need to be taught with explicit, whole-group instruction. The interactive whiteboard is better suited for this type of instruction. Correct modeling and working sample problems are how foundations are built. Young students are also more active and need to use their bodies to learn; a tablet cannot provide that venue for large muscle movement. The interactive whiteboard continues to be an effective, relevant classroom tool, especially for early elementary grades.

In education, the ultimate goal is for students to learn the curriculum in a safe and supportive environment. An interactive whiteboard can help achieve this goal. In addition to making difficult material easier for students to learn, a teacher's effective use of the IWB motivates students and can help manage groups of students by implementing the board's attention-grabbing features. An interactive whiteboard also increases students' ability to memorize and retain the material.

If an interactive whiteboard is available in your school building and some teachers have not taken advantage of its fullest potential, provide them some support, or kindly ask them to step aside so you can offer a simple demonstration. A fun and sleek teaching tool should not sit idly by as a display board or as something that garners resentment. Those interactive boards were made to be interacted with. Use them to their fullest potential!

REFERENCES

British Educational Communications and Technology Agency (BECTA). (2007). What the research says about interactive whiteboards. Retrieved from http://dera.ioe.ac.uk/5318/

Bunce, D. M., Flens, E. A., & Neiles, K. Y. (2010). How long can students pay attention in class? A study of student attention decline using clickers. *Journal of Chemical Education 87*, 1438–43.

Gardner, H. (1983). *Frames of mind*. New York, NY: Basic Books.

Marzano, R. J., & Haystead, M. (2009). *Final report on the evaluation of the Promethean technology*. Englewood, CO: Marzano Research Laboratory.

Sigman, A. (2010, September). *Teletubbies is as bad for your child as a violent video game, says leading psychologist*. Retrieved from www.dailymail. co.uk/health/article-1311139/Teletubbiesbad-child-violent-video-games.html#ixzz2PQNYVYDH

NATIONAL EDUCATIONAL TECHNOLOGY STANDARDS

National Educational Technology Standards for Students (NETS•S)

All K–12 students should be prepared to meet the following standards and performance indicators.

1. Creativity and Innovation

Students demonstrate creative thinking, construct knowledge, and develop innovative products and processes using technology. Students:

    a. apply existing knowledge to generate new ideas, products, or processes

    b. create original works as a means of personal or group expression

    c. use models and simulations to explore complex systems and issues

    d. identify trends and forecast possibilities

2. **Communication and Collaboration**

   Students use digital media and environments to communicate and work collaboratively, including at a distance, to support individual learning and contribute to the learning of others. Students:

   a. interact, collaborate, and publish with peers, experts, or others employing a variety of digital environments and media

   b. communicate information and ideas effectively to multiple audiences using a variety of media and formats

   c. develop cultural understanding and global awareness by engaging with learners of other cultures

   d. contribute to project teams to produce original works or solve problems

3. **Research and Information Fluency**

   Students apply digital tools to gather, evaluate, and use information. Students:

   a. plan strategies to guide inquiry

   b. locate, organize, analyze, evaluate, synthesize, and ethically use information from a variety of sources and media

   c. evaluate and select information sources and digital tools based on the appropriateness to specific tasks

   d. process data and report results

4. **Critical Thinking, Problem Solving, and Decision Making**

Students use critical-thinking skills to plan and conduct research, manage projects, solve problems, and make informed decisions using appropriate digital tools and resources. Students:

   a. identify and define authentic problems and significant questions for investigation

   b. plan and manage activities to develop a solution or complete a project

   c. collect and analyze data to identify solutions and make informed decisions

   d. use multiple processes and diverse perspectives to explore alternative solutions

5. **Digital Citizenship**

Students understand human, cultural, and societal issues related to technology and practice legal and ethical behavior. Students:

   a. advocate and practice the safe, legal, and responsible use of information and technology

   b. exhibit a positive attitude toward using technology that supports collaboration, learning, and productivity

   c. demonstrate personal responsibility for lifelong learning

   d. exhibit leadership for digital citizenship

6. Technology Operations and Concepts

Students demonstrate a sound understanding of technology concepts, systems, and operations. Students:

a. understand and use technology systems

b. select and use applications effectively and productively

c. troubleshoot systems and applications

d. transfer current knowledge to the learning of new technologies

National Educational Technology Standards for Teachers (NETS•T)

All classroom teachers should be prepared to meet the following standards and performance indicators.

1. Facilitate and Inspire Student Learning and Creativity

Teachers use their knowledge of subject matter, teaching and learning, and technology to facilitate experiences that advance student learning, creativity, and innovation in both face-to-face and virtual environments. Teachers:

a. promote, support, and model creative and innovative thinking and inventiveness

b. engage students in exploring real-world issues and solving authentic problems using digital tools and resources

c. promote student reflection using collaborative tools to reveal and clarify students' conceptual understanding and thinking, planning, and creative processes

d. model collaborative knowledge construction by engaging in learning with students, colleagues, and others in face-to-face and virtual environments

2. Design and Develop Digital-Age Learning Experiences and Assessments

Teachers design, develop, and evaluate authentic learning experiences and assessments incorporating contemporary tools and resources to maximize content learning in context and to develop the knowledge, skills, and attitudes identified in the NETS•S. Teachers:

a. design or adapt relevant learning experiences that incorporate digital tools and resources to promote student learning and creativity

b. develop technology-enriched learning environments that enable all students to pursue their individual curiosities and become active participants in setting their own educational goals, managing their own learning, and assessing their own progress

c. customize and personalize learning activities to address students' diverse learning styles, working strategies, and abilities using digital tools and resources

d. provide students with multiple and varied formative and summative assessments aligned with content and technology standards and use resulting data to inform learning and teaching

3. Model Digital-Age Work and Learning

Teachers exhibit knowledge, skills, and work processes representative of an innovative professional in a global and digital society. Teachers:

a. demonstrate fluency in technology systems and the transfer of current knowledge to new technologies and situations

b. collaborate with students, peers, parents, and community members using digital tools and resources to support student success and innovation

c. communicate relevant information and ideas effectively to students, parents, and peers using a variety of digital-age media and formats

d. model and facilitate effective use of current and emerging digital tools to locate, analyze, evaluate, and use information resources to support research and learning

4. Promote and Model Digital Citizenship and Responsibility

Teachers understand local and global societal issues and responsibilities in an evolving digital culture and exhibit legal and ethical behavior in their professional practices. Teachers:

a. advocate, model, and teach safe, legal, and ethical use of digital information and technology, including respect for copyright, intellectual property, and the appropriate documentation of sources

b. address the diverse needs of all learners by using learner-centered strategies and providing equitable access to appropriate digital tools and resources

c. promote and model digital etiquette and responsible social interactions related to the use of technology and information

d. develop and model cultural understanding and global awareness by engaging with colleagues and students of other cultures using digital-age communication and collaboration tools

5. Engage in Professional Growth and Leadership

Teachers continuously improve their professional practice, model lifelong learning, and exhibit leadership in their school and professional community by promoting and demonstrating the effective use of digital tools and resources. Teachers:

a. participate in local and global learning communities to explore creative applications of technology to improve student learning

b. exhibit leadership by demonstrating a vision of technology infusion, participating in shared decision making and community building, and developing the leadership and technology skills of others

c. evaluate and reflect on current research and professional practice on a regular basis to make effective use of existing and emerging digital tools and resources in support of student learning

d. contribute to the effectiveness, vitality, and self-renewal of the teaching profession and of their school and community

© 2008 International Society for Technology in Education (ISTE), www.iste.org. All rights reserved.

INDEX

A

ABCya, 46
achievement, student, 1, 33–35, 94
active learning, 24–25
addition, 67, 68, 71, 72
adjectives, 61, 62
administrators, educational, 91
algebraic thinking and operations, 67–68, 70–71, 72, 74–75
alphabet, 36, 55–56
animal habitats, 77
Animoto, 50
Arcademic Skill Builders, 46
Armored Penguin, 52
arms, 10
Assign-A-Day, 52
assistive technology, 30
attendance, student, 35
attendance taking, 81
auditory learners, 27–28

B

base ten, number and operations in, 72–73
BBC Learning Schools, 46
BECTA (British Educational Communications and Technology Agency), 33–34
Befuddlr, 50
behavioral management tools, 31
benefits of interactive technology
  classroom management, 30–31, 93–94
  differentiated instruction, 25–29
  resources, leveraging limited, 32
  scaffolding, 29–30
  shared learning, 32

student achievement, 1, 33–35, 94
student engagement, 1, 24–25
student motivation, 1–2, 35–37, 93
teacher motivation, 37–38
technology standards, meeting, 38–40
big books, 43
Bluetooth, 8
boards. See also interactive whiteboards (IWBs)
  hard-surfaced, 9
  height of, 17
  soft-surfaced, 13
books, 42–43
booms, 10
British Educational Communications and Technology Agency (BECTA), 33–34
bubbl.us, 50

C

cabling, 8
calendar time, 69, 81
capture technology, 14
cardinality and counting, 64–67
carts, rollable, 13
ceiling-mounted projectors, 11–12
cheerleaders, 90–91
classroom management, 30–31, 93–94
coin values, 73
color, 44
color mixing, 78
color sort, 75